American
in Disguise

American in Disguise

DANIEL I. OKIMOTO

with a foreword by
JAMES A. MICHENER

A Weatherhill Book
WALKER/WEATHERHILL, *New York & Tokyo*

First Edition, 1971

Published by JOHN WEATHERHILL, INC., *of New York and Tokyo, with editorial offices at 7-6-13 Roppongi, Minato-ku, Tokyo 106. Distributed in the United States by* WALKER AND COMPANY, *720 Fifth Avenue, New York City 10019. Copyright in Japan, 1970 by John Weatherhill, Inc.; all rights reserved. Printed in Japan.*

LCC Card No. 70–121065   ISBN 0-8027-2438-8

Dedicated in love, respect, and gratitude
to the memory of my father
TAMEICHI OKIMOTO

Contents

Foreword

ONE OF THE MOST vivid memories of my life is that rainy midnight when a nearly empty China Air Transport plane flew into Iwakuni Airport, at the southern end of Honshu, and deposited my newly married wife and me on Japanese soil for her first visit and my nineteenth. She was an American nisei—Mari Yoriko Sabusawa from Colorado—and I was suddenly apprehensive lest she find the homeland of her parents less appealing that I myself found it.

"Remember," I warned her as we were about to descend the steps, "you are visiting *my* country, and I don't want to hear any remarks about 'the funny little people.' "

We drove that night into Hiroshima in the car of Oliver Statler, who was more Japanese than either of us, and for the next week Statler and I had the extreme pleasure of introducing Japan to a Japanese. Apart from an excellent familiarity with the language, which my wife had studiously acquired in a Japanese after-hours school in Colorado, Statler and I knew so much more about Japan than she did that there was really no comparison, and we were both much relieved when we found her responding to the

ix

new land. We desperately wanted her to like it, because Japan is a country well worth affection. My wife never became as Japanese as I, but at least she made an honest effort to understand the land from which her family had sprung, and for this I was thankful.

I recalled that experience when reading this book. Daniel Okimoto was born in the Japanese concentration center at the Santa Anita Racetrack at the same time my wife was interned there. Many American wives boast of ancestors who came over on the ship following the *Mayflower*—the overload was tremendous—or of grandfathers who were governors or senators of proud old states. Mine has a unique boast: "I was imprisoned in the stable used by Equipoise." Okimoto, therefore, is one of the first nisei born in the course of World War II, or later, to write of his experiences. He is thus unique, and what he has to say fills a gap in our knowledge.

We have had many accounts of issei who fought the good fight in California in the early days and educated their children at great hardship; my father-in-law was one of the best. And we have had excellent accounts of nisei born in the 1915–25 period who suffered indignities and imprisonment because they happened to be Japanese, and who then volunteered for battle service overseas, bringing themselves and their group much distinction; Daniel Inouye's book is a case in point. But this is the first book I've seen by someone who grew up in the postwar world and experienced America afresh after the great dislocations of 1941. It has much to tell us and will be for many years a valued document of the genesis of Japanese-American attitudes.

At some points the book goes over familiar ground, as in

the story of the evacuation, but in doing so it often throws up startling new facts, or at least facts with which I was not familiar, as in Okimoto's observation that in the order which dispossessed the Japanese Americans of their liberty and possessions, the government could not bring itself to say the order applied to American citizens as well as to Japanese and instead spoke of "whether aliens or non-aliens." What a hideous circumlocution! What in hell is a nonalien? What could he possibly be but a citizen? I had read this pompous phrase years ago without catching its irony; I am grateful to Okimoto for having clarified the matter for me. Next time we come up with a beautiful and flashy substitute for real words I hope I catch it.

As a matter of fact, I may have improved somewhat in this respect. When the My-Lai shootings hit the headlines I was revolted to find that the United States Army was reprimanding its soldiers for having shot "Asian person-nel"—meaning men—and "Asians"—meaning women—as if these designations made murder less reprehensible.

One of the finest aspects of this book is Okimoto's sober analysis of the comparisons between the Japanese experience with racial intolerance and that of the Negro. He has some very good things to say on this subject, things which all Japanese and Chinese Americans ought to keep in mind, as well as Irishmen and Russians. It is not just for one of these other immigrant groups to say, "We made it, so why can't the Negro?" There is no comparison, because the Japanese from Hiroshima who came to California and the Lithuanian Jew who came to New York brought with them a tradition of learning, a powerful religion suited to their needs, a total way of life which, if it could not be transplanted wholly to a new setting, could at least provide a stable set of values that would keep the family together and the children organized until the new culture of America could graft itself upon the old. The Japanese immigrant, as Okimoto's account of his father and mother proves, came to America with abundant spiritual and cultural riches; here they developed them.

But, most crucial of all, the Japanese and the Jews and the Irish and the Chinese were never slaves. They were different, and they were often persecuted for this difference, but they were never stigmatized with having been slaves, moved about as chattel, and deprived of the stable family life they had known in the old countries. And that is a difference so profound that it ill behooves the other immigrant groups to demand of the Negro that he perform as they did. The rules are different.

I was surprised by Okimoto's account of his family's attempt to rent a house in Pasadena as late as 1954. I had never given the subject much thought, but I had supposed that by then anti-Japanese emotions had largely died down and I was not prepared for the struggle the Okimoto family had in finding a place to live, nor for the reception their youngest son, Daniel, had when he reported to an all-white school. He tells a shocking story, and I suppose it is being repeated even today, somewhere in the United States. Books like his and protests from whites like me are the way we diminish these situations. I would hope that by the year 2010 such events will have disappeared, but I doubt that they will vanish much sooner.

I found particularly helpful Okimoto's account of his years at Tokyo University, for they came at the height of student troubles there and his insights into what happened can be useful to us who are perplexed about what do do with the student uprisings that are occurring in the United States. The Japanese experience was not a pretty one, nor was it fruitful, as Okimoto points out.

One of the most interesting sections of this book is the brief one dealing with the differences between the Japanese who chose to exile themselves in South America and those who came to North America. The former became Catholic, freer in their social patterns, more relaxed in dress, while the latter became Protestants, strongly inhibited socially and conformist in dress. I wish the author had given us more material on this subject, for it is one worth investigation.

The most constructive aspect of the book is that although the author went to Japan, he also returned to the United States, and the value of his work is that he sees himself in both mirrors. This is therefore a book not merely about a young Japanese American with a sophisticated Princeton-Harvard education seeing his parents' homeland for the first time; it is also a book about America, as seen by an American with an out-of-the-ordinary experiential background. He casts a new light on an old society.

For some years my wife has had the rowdy habit, when Caucasians irritate her with condescension, of saying, "I am writing a book. I'm calling it *America Through Slanted Eyes*." This startles some people, amuses those who recognize it as a joke.

Daniel Okimoto has not written such a book, and I suppose no one else should, either. He has written as an American, as a man responsible for the character of his society. I wonder if he doesn't brood a little too much upon the grievances of his youth, but I have found that no outsider can advise another as to how the latter should interpret the experiences of his past. If Okimoto needs to feel that at Pasadena he was grievously maltreated, and if from this conviction he gets the strength to persevere to Princeton and to Harvard and to Tokyo University—it's about ten times as difficult to get into the latter and carries much more prestige—then he has put his Pasedena experience to good account. And if an accumulation of irritations led him to write this book, then that is a very good use to which to put irritations. On the whole he has handled this difficult problem of balance commendably.

The last chapter, dealing with his marriage to a girl "from a middle-class, Anglo-Saxon family in Idaho," is a sensible statement on the problem of interracial marriage. As one who is engaged in such a marriage and who has experienced never one hour of tension from it, I wish the author and his wife well. As a matter of fact, I suppose it's much better that the husband in such a marriage be Oriental and the wife Caucasian. To have it the other way poses certain problems in that tradition says the Japanese wife is quiet, submissive, and subservient. It took me several years to discover that not one of those adjectives applies, and I am still looking for that clown who wrote the novel about how the Japanese wife allows her husband to be king when he comes home from work.

JAMES A. MICHENER

Acknowledgments

The process of writing a book, as I have discovered, is commonly a collaborative endeavor rather than a strictly individual enterprise. Although only the name of the author appears on the finished product, there is generally a long list of people who, at various stages, have contributed vitally to the shaping of the manuscript. It is a pleasure here to give proper acknowledgement to a few of those individuals who have worked diligently for the publication of this book. My thanks go to the very capable editorial staff at John Weatherhill, Inc. I wish also to record my indebtedness to members of my family without whom, of course, this story could never have been written. And finally, my deep appreciation goes to my wife, Nancy, whose contributions extend beyond concrete and vast improvements of the manuscript to warm support and constant encouragement, in the absence of which I might several times have abandoned this effort.

Ann Arbor, Michigan, 1970

American
in Disguise

Prologue

MORE EXCITED THAN I had expected, I hurried toward the group of relatives standing in the waiting room of Haneda, Tokyo's international airport. I had put one arm out ready to shake hands but those waiting greeted me with a flurry of deep bows. Embarrassed, and unaccustomed to the Japanese style of greeting, I tried, awkwardly I now see, to respond in kind. This brought on more bowing, which I matched as best as I could, perhaps compelled by the desire to show proper Oriental respect to my elders. For a full five minutes, then, during my first face-to-face meeting with my grandfather, grandmother, cousins, and other relatives, I was bent stiffly over, eyes taking in only the scuffed tops of my shoes, not the faces I had come thousands of miles to see. It was for me an odd, frustrating way of showing the emotion I felt, for I had looked forward to this moment for a long time.

Born during World War II, not long after my parents' immigration to the United States, I had grown up without personal contact with relatives aside from my immediate family, and largely without any real knowledge of the country that was the homeland of my Asian ancestors. Even though this first meeting was unsettling, the experience of actually being in Japan and with family was unforgettable. Whatever poise I might have mustered under other circumstances deserted me and I could scarcely say an intelligible sentence in the elementary Japanese I had learned at Princeton, much less match the complicated and exquisite politeness being shown me.

And there was so much I wanted to say about my hopes, dreams, and expectations—I was eager also to know my relatives, to see how they lived, to understand what they thought, to form a picture of how my own life might have been had I been born and reared in Japan. And I wanted to hear of my parents' lives before they left for America, to comprehend the circumstances of their departure, to discover, in short, the vast and as yet unexplored world of my ancestral past.

A second-generation American of Japanese descent, for the first time in the land of his forefathers, I wondered how I would react to a postwar Japan unknown to either my parents or my brothers and sister. What would I find familiar? What different? Would the impressions gained alter substantially myself and my world view? Could I, and how would I, fit in? These questions were not idle ones, but touched upon matters of intense personal importance connected with the sensitive issue of self-identity, as I had profoundly ambivalent feelings about the Japanese aspect of myself. Firsthand experiences in the United States with racial prejudice, which said in effect that being Japanese was to be somehow inferior, had made it difficult to evaluate, still less fully accept, the role of my Japanese heritage in my life as an American. When I looked at myself, I felt a curious mixture of pride and contempt, of satisfaction and discontent, of security and anxiety. Indeed for much of my life, I had struggled with the conviction that I was an American in disguise, a creature part of, yet somehow detached from, the mainstream of American society.

This sense of alienation had been a fact of my life from its very beginning, as I was born, the last son of immigrant parents, in the stables of a racetrack in Southern California designated as a transfer point for those Japanese on the West Coast who were being herded into wartime internment camps. Long after the geographical isolation of internment had ended, a strong feeling of psychological distance from white American society persisted. This feeling was reinforced through antagonisms growing out of racial preconceptions on the part of the white majority, and the disquieting notion grew that I and others of my kind were only partial Americans. Our physical characteristics made a kind of mask that prevented the "others" (as we thought of them) from seeing us as we truly were. A common experience for us nisei* was to be introduced as Japanese, with no mention of the fact that by virtue of birth we were Americans.

In my own case, I had drawn from my Japanese legacy a certain sense of security, a drive to social success, and a measure of pride in the achievements against great odds of one minority within American society, but the obstacles to

---

*Nisei is the term for second-generation children of Japanese immigrants, who themselves are known as issei. The third generation is sansei, the fourth yonsei. In this book I use nisei as an all-inclusive category for the American-born offspring of the issei, be they second, third, or fourth generation. Differences of outlook and age have been indicated by dividing Japanese Americans broadly into prewar and postwar groups, the last including those, like myself, who were born during World War II.

complete assimilation were formidable, for one was a strange animal, not easily asorbed into the complex social patterns of the United States. The worst result of this situation was that I became deeply vulnerable to the assumptions underlying racist attitudes, and was beset by a fear that they were correct. When others called me "Little Nip" or "Slant Eyes," I usually purged the pain away by laughing. When I was a child and my toys from Japan broke, I was told that the Japanese were no more than a race of imitators who could produce only cheap, second-rate goods. In movies showing scenes from World War II, I learned that the sinister "Japs" taking such sadistic pleasure in killing and torturing almost uniformly brave American soldiers were representative of a whole nation, and I, although of Japanese descent, was expected to share this popular view. It is not perhaps surprising that I tried as best I could to disassociate myself from "bad" Japanese in as many ways as possible, for I wanted to be above all an "American," whatever meaning that may have had. But this attempt was doomed to failure, for I was not after all representative of the central figure of middle-class American mythology, the WASP in all his white-skinned, blue-eyed glory. In spite of that I *was* American and hardly knew whether to love or hate that which I was and wanted to be.

Much later, during my three-year residence in Japan, the ambivalence within became alarmingly active. My reactions to Japan and its people oscillated wildly from extremes of euphoric infatuation to outright distaste. I was not experiencing Japan objectively, for each time that I recognized something of myself in the Japanese situation, I was drawn back into the tangled bundle of feelings that had grown out of my life as a nisei in the United States. Yet gradually I gained a badly needed perspective upon my dual heritage and a clearer vision of what constituted my own personal identity.

In Japan I came to see how strongly my American conditioning had left me ill-equipped to cope with the land of my ancestors. For example, I at first was strongly critical of the physical appearance of the Japanese. The men were, by white American standards, short and skinny; the women plain and thick-legged. Those women who seemed beautiful to me were precisely the ones who most closely resembled Caucasians. I disliked particularly what seemed to me—the pseudo-Caucasian—eyes that were too thin, too narrow, even though my own eyes have the full and tight epicanthic fold that makes Japanese eyes seem small to Westerners. As I lived longer in Japan I realized what was happening: that out of my own self-hatred I was judging by borrowed standards, and this in itself was a stunning revelation that contributed much to a growing awareness of my true self.

In more complex ways, the interaction with the fascinating culture of Japan provided invaluable insights to my understanding of America's nisei subculture. I was able to discern after a time threads of continuity between the mother country and its offspring in the United States. Some of the characterstics that made possible Japan's spectacular reconstruction and growth after the war were the same as those found among issei and nisei—adherence to a close family unit, a stress on education at all costs, the high value of hard work and frugality, the sense of community, qualities of patience and forebearance, and a relentless drive to social success. At the same time, I came to understand events that had long puzzled me—the

Japanese-American lack of resistance to internment, the issei-nisei community's political passivity, its failure to participate in civil-rights movements, its general acceptance of a status quo defined by those not only outside the community but often actively despising it. Viewed from Japan the American nisei experience was thrown into sharp relief, and the strengths and weaknesses (many of which I share) of Japanese Americans stood out strongly.

Time and space now separate me from that initial and—as I look back now—quintessential meeting in Haneda Airport. The awkward, troubled youth is gone, and the person he has become is able, or at best thinks himself able, to deal with a complex heritage with at least a minimum of objective skill. But the story of that youth, of his family, his community, and the dual heritage that created an American in disguise does, I believe, have meaning in a world where minorities are in revolt, values are ceaselessly being critically examined, and the whole problem of identity has become one of the central issues of our time.

1

Journey
to America

IT WAS IN THE summer of 1937 that Tameichi and Kirie Okimoto leaned over the ship's railing, straining to look beyond the sunshine sparkle of the sea at the vast expanse of land looming into view. As the ship moved slowly into the southern California port of San Pedro, the Okimotos could scarcely contain their excitement as they rushed about collecting luggage. For them and their two infant children, arrival in America represented much more than the end of a twenty-day sea voyage. It was the culmination of a decision to emigrate from Japan and the start of a fresh, new life in the United States—fabled haven for poor, oppressed immigrants, Promised Land of justice and liberty.

Five years later, in the spring of 1942, Tameichi Okimoto, his three young children and pregnant wife stood next to a small pile of suitcases and boxes, the sum total of their worldly possessions, surveying the unfamiliar compounds of the famous Santa Anita Racetrack. These ministers of the Lord had not been seduced into becoming racing fans, nor

9

had they come here to save others from hedonistic vices. In an aberrant twist of history this playground of wealthy, freewheeling sportsmen had been converted into a way station for thousands of Japanese Americans on the West Coast, who, by virtue of birth or descent, were about to be banished to wartime internment camps. The compound, glutted with barracks hastily thrown up to accommodate the large transient population, was fenced off and patrolled by armed soldiers. There, amid the crowds and confusion, the Okimoto family faced a disillusioning dénouement to their hopes for America: they were prisoners in the Promised Land.

Military imprisonment was particularly ironic for Tameichi Okimoto because the sequence of events that led him to America had begun with his aversion for militarism. Born in Yamaguchi Prefecture in 1904, the only son in a military family, he had been raised in Taiwan and Korea, then colonies in the Japanese empire. His family's involvement in army matters was far-reaching. One uncle, a highly decorated brigadier general named Morinaga, had been one of Chiang Kai-shek's instructors in Japan. A number of Tameichi's cousins had attended the prestigious Army Academy (the equivalent of West Point) on their way to becoming high-ranking career officers.

Despite family tradition and the rapid route to power offered by a professional military career, Tameichi refused to be swept up in the fervor of ultranationalism and military expansionism. Shinto, the religious-political underpinning of Japan's schemes for a Greater East Asia Co-Prosperity Sphere, struck him as being fanatical, intellectually insulting, and spiritually bankrupt. Despite threats of disinheritance, he turned away from military service. Haunted by an aching sense of discontent, he returned to farming relatives in Iwakuni (just outside Hiroshima) who offered him a plot of land to till. Tameichi rejected the rights to the land, not wanting to remain permanently in the country. Instead he struck out for Tokyo, determined to carve out a life for himself without having to rely on his family.

In Tokyo his personal odyssey for a time was barren and without direction. Able to find only menial work, Tameichi felt his future was without hope; the deep spiritual vacuum inside, it seemed, would never be filled. After several months of Spartan living he fell critically ill of pneumonia.

He was without money for proper medical treatment and so he sought help from a Christian church where a missionary took him into his care. For several months he received medical treatment along with instruction in the Christian religion. The teachings of the Bible were quite foreign to him; facets of the Western religion eluded him: the elaborate theology, the concept of original sin, the notions of damnation and redemption. But many aspects of Christianity impressed him greatly: its social and ethical wisdom, its literary beauty, its decisive impact on Western civilization. His receptivity to the religion was heightened by his spiritual gropings and a profound sense of gratitude toward the kindly missionary. By the time he recovered fully from his illness, Tameichi felt he had found at last his life's calling. From the doorstep of death and spiritual starvation he dedicated himself to the service of God through the ministry.

At a theological seminary in Tokyo, Tameichi Okimoto met another convert bent upon becoming a minister. Her name was Kirie Kumagai, a cheerful, warm, oval-faced woman three years older than he. A native of Fukuoka,

Kyushu, Kirie was the youngest of six children in a farming family. Being both intellectually curious and singularly stubborn, she had overcome parental opposition and powerful social disapproval of "overly educated" women to gain a college education.

After teaching a few years, a change was precipitated in her life by the sudden death of her beloved father. Because Kirie had always felt especially close to him, the unexpected passing not only left her in a state of semishock but also in total bewilderment about life. How could death so cruelly take away so gentle a man? What meaning would life have without him? Deprived of a central focal point of her being, Kirie suffered a complete identity crisis.

During this time she, like Tameichi Okimoto, fell under the influence of a Christian missionary who extended sympathy and understanding when it was needed most. Although Kirie too could not understand all the sophisticated concepts of the religion, she was consoled by the idea of a heavenly afterlife and found in the omnipotent God of Christianity the magnetic figure of fatherly love she longed for.

The Kumagai family, however, took a dim view of their youngest child's newly found faith. They tried repeatedly, without success, to persuade her to abandon the foreign religion. It was bringing shame upon the family, and shame in a small rural community in Japan was hard to live down. In the end they issued an ultimatum: either give up Christianity or leave the household in disgrace. Kirie chose to retain her faith.

Following a period of intense introspection and study, she enrolled in a theological seminary to prepare for the ministry, along with her classmate Tameichi Okimoto.

After graduation the two were married. Though Kirie was slightly older, the match was fitting in view of the common background of iconoclasm, alienation from family, and dedication to their chosen occupations.

In 1937 the Okimotos were approached by the Oriental Missionary Society about going to the United States to serve among the large number of Japanese immigrants. After careful deliberation they accepted the request. Leaving Japan, where less than one percent of the population was Christian, to cross the Pacific as missionaries to America where the large majority were Christian seemed to them a curious reversal of fate. But they believed it to be God's will and were eager to settle in America, where they believed they could raise their children in a Christian nation under a democratic, liberty-loving government.

Five years later this same government stripped them and their people of freedom and human rights and sentenced them to exile in the wilderness. Standing on the grounds of what the government called the Santa Anita Assembly Center, the Okimotos tried to comfort their three small children. Of the five, Mrs. Okimoto, her stomach bulging with child, showed the most obvious signs of strain. The train ride had been wearing. She was worried that the long trip might have affected the baby growing within her; having suffered two miscarriages before, she feared yet another. Had she and her husband only known what lay ahead, they would have tried harder to avoid a fourth child. Conception was a mistake as it was. With the future of the Japanese people in America so dark and uncertain, she wondered whether God would not spare this baby the pain of facing a life with so little apparent hope. In the process of being shunted off to internment camps under armed escort, the Okimotos were beginning to have doubts about their decision to leave Japan. Had they misunderstood the will of God?

Three and one-half months passed in Santa Anita. Already mid-August, the summer heat passed straight through the paper-thin barrack walls, raising beads of perspiration on Kirie Okimoto's swollen body. The smell of the stables was at its worst during the heat and sleep was uneasy with delivery near. Around 3:00 A.M. she felt a succession of familiar pains; rousing her husband, she immediately rushed down to the makeshift camp hospital. Six hours later, at 9:05 A.M., August 14, 1942, amid the smelly stables, a son was born.

The noisy, hungry boy was without a name for a few days. The three older children had been christened with first names from figures the parents admired in the Bible, followed by Japanese middle names: their eldest son was Paul Mitsuru; their daughter, Ruth Yoshiko; and their second son, Joseph Tsutomu.

The matter of selecting a name for the last son was important to the Okimotos in view of the circumstances of his birth. They wanted something which captured the adversity of the situation, a name that suggested suffering yet carried some reassurance for the future. The story of Daniel in the lions' den was brought to mind all too vividly by the way the Japanese were being thrown into detention camps. Gripped by fears about the fate of all Japanese in America, the Okimoto couple agreed on the name Daniel Iwao.

2

Prisoners

THE CHAIN OF EVENTS that brought the Okimotos to Santa Anita began during the panic-stricken months following the surprise assault on Pearl Harbor and against the background of all-out war. But the causes of the evacuation can be traced back to the anti-Oriental sentiment that was directed first against Chinese immigrants in the mid-nineteenth century. Resentment against "cheap coolie labor" produced a popular image of the Chinese as immoral and treacherous—not fit for human company. When Japanese began arriving in substantial numbers after 1890, it was easy enough to have this image extended to them. "Now the Jap is a wily an' a crafty individual—more so than the Chink," warned one writer in the *Sacramento Bee*. "They are lower in the scale of civilization than the whites and will never become our equals."

During the early decades of the twentieth century racial prejudice on the West Coast took on the characteristics of an anti-Japanese movement, first among labor unions anxious to eliminate cheap Japanese labor, then among various civic and pressure groups such as branches of the American Legion, the Native Sons of the Golden West,

15

and the California Farm Bureau Federation, which were eager to protect the West Coast from the "contaminating" influence of Orientals. As Japan flexed its military muscles in Korea, China, and Russia, concern came to be focused on the so-called Yellow Peril, which to some hyperactive imaginations meant the overrunning of the West Coast by Japanese or the invasion of the U.S. mainland by the Imperial Japanese Army.

To cope with these fancied threats, certain control measures were deemed necessary. Organized anti-Japanese pressure was instrumental in the passage of a variety of discriminatory measures, aimed at curbing immigration and checking threats of social advance. The first of these was the Gentlemen's Agreement (1908) by which Japan promised voluntarily to restrict the flow of immigration. This was followed by the Alien Land Law (1913) which prohibited the predominantly rural Japanese not only from owning and bequeathing land but also from leasing land for any period over three years. As is clear from the statement of one high-ranking California official, the Alien Land Law was clearly intended to discourage the Japanese from coming and settling in the U.S., because "they will not come in large numbers and long abide with us if they may not acquire land." When this legislation failed to achieve its avowed purpose, an amendment was secured in 1920, depriving the Japanese of the right even to lease agricultural land. Four years later, in 1924, the Immigration Exclusion Act was passed, virtually barring the Japanese from any further settlement in America. Judged unfit for citizenship, treated as the scum of the West, harassed by a battery of legal restrictions, the Japanese in America were subjected to a degree of discrimination that was in many ways similar to that directed against American blacks.

Yet, owing largely to cultural characteristics carried over from rural Japan, the issei immigrants endured this debasement in silence. Efforts to hamper or suppress them merely brought out certain qualities—like perseverance and industry—which motivated them to work even more diligently. Countless numbers of farmers went through a pattern which became familiar: they started out as cheap hired hands, worked ceaselessly, endured hardships, saved money, and eventually got around legal barriers against ownership by purchasing land in the names of their American-born children. To accumulate enough money to buy a small plot of property usually required a lifetime of unrelenting work, yet these immigrants were willing to pay this price so their children could start out with the kind of advantages—land, homes, money—they never had. Japanese families in America were bound closely together, especially by the mothers, just as their communities tended to be tightly knit by common backgrounds, goals, and anti-Japanese hostility.

It was not unusual for the issei to live their lives for, and later pin their hopes on, their children. Even though their lot was incredibly hard and their status low, most never lost hope that things would be different for their children. Hence, after purchasing land, they continued to endure the harsh toil so as to be able to give their children what they considered the key to success: a college education. So highly was education esteemed within the Japanese community that few sacrifices were considered too great for it. To be sure, social mobility even for college-educated nisei remained restricted during the prewar period, but most parents felt the situation had become more promising.

The closeness of the family unit, tightness of the ethnic community, and strength of value priorities worked together splendidly in conditioning the first- and second-generation Japanese to adapt to an alien society, even one as ridden with racist hostilities as America is. Within his home environment the nisei would typically be told to set ambitious goals, respect his teachers, study hard, earn good grades, succeed in his occupation, and in so doing repay his parents a tiny measure for the enormous sacrifices they made on his behalf. At the same time home values were reinforced by those of the community. The same nisei boy was expected to endure prejudice uncomplainingly, conform to American norms unquestioningly, rise as high as possible socially, set a good example constantly, and hence bring honor not only to his family but to his whole sub-culture. Social deviation—crime, personal rebellion, or nonconformity—was usually penalized strongly so as to make the nisei feel that he was overbearingly unfilial toward his parents as well as to shame him before everyone in the tiny Japanese-American society.

The successes of the Japanese in America threatened to come to naught after the Japanese air squadron swept down on Pearl Harbor. The suddenness of the attack confirmed belief in the stereotype of the Japanese as devious people and fanned flames of suspect loyalty that had been smoldering over the years. Any air attack so well planned and executed, it was blithely assumed, *must* have been aided by subversive activities of the large (over 200,000) Japanese population in Hawaii. Unconfirmed news reports of fifth-column activities—such as cutting arrow-shaped lanes in the cane fields to guide the fighter planes, and throwing up road blocks to impede military counteroperations—hit some of the presses, giving rise to widespread alarm among the Pacific coast population.

With Japanese concentrated near key harbor and airfield areas on the mainland, there was a great deal of concern that a repetition of Pearl Harbor might occur as well in California. Such fears raced out of hand as Japanese submarines were said to be off the shores of California and ham radio operators swore strange messages were being signaled from the mainland to these enemy vessels. Secret repositories of arms and communications equipment were reportedly uncovered in the homes of some Japanese residents.

No matter how vehemently sympathy for the enemy cause was disclaimed or instances of subversion disproved, the Japanese in America simply could not escape the stigma of nearly a century of racist paranoia abruptly rekindled by Pearl Harbor. Objectivity, even among some people noted for just attitudes, seemed to get lost in the rapidly growing hysteria. One "reputable" newsman charged that ninety percent of the Japanese in California were loyal to Japan, without bothering to make any investigation. "They will die joyously," he confidently predicted, "for the honor of Japan." Government officials, like Earl Warren, then attorney general of California, also suspected subversion on the part of the Japanese, going so far as to interpret the utter lack of sabotage as evidence that it would soon break out. The Japanese, many thought, while pretending to be loyal, were really waiting for the right moment to act.

The atmosphere became so emotionally charged because of daily broadcasts of successive enemy victories in the Pacific that it was dangerous for Japanese to walk the streets in certain areas along the West Coast. Some were assaulted by marauding gangs of superpatriots; others were knifed or shot coldly in public. Cries for the internment of all Japanese descendants rose to a fevered pitch during the months of January and February 1942. A minority of alarmists swung popular feeling toward an attitude of "better safe than sorry" regarding the proposal to concentrate Japanese in isolated camps.

The mass media, normally an essential mechanism for the smooth functioning of a democratic form of government, became a tool in the movement to deprive an American minority of its inherent and legal perogatives. One reporter for the Hearst newspapers, for example, wrote: "I am for the immediate removal of every Japanese on the West Coast to a point deep in the interior. I don't mean a nice part of the interior either. Herd 'em up, pack 'em off, and give them the inside room in the badlands. Let 'em be pinched, hurt, hungry, and dead up against it. . . . Personally, I hate the Japanese. And that goes for all of them."

Pressure groups and civic organizations also threw their weight behind the internment campaign. Branches of the superpatriotic American Legion, which prided themselves on their dedication to protect the "American heritage," agitated actively for evacuation, forgetting that immigration from abroad, human liberty, and individual rights were essential features of that heritage. Agricultural groups, which had long sought to suppress Japanese farmers, were particularly active in the movement because, apart from the imagined dangers of subversion, removal of the Japanese was a convenient way of eliminating competition. Other rabid groups, like the American League, the Anti-Japanese League, and the Ban the Japs Committee, were formed to lobby for immediate relocation.

It made no difference whether a Japanese was an American citizen or not; the color of his skin and the shape of his eyes constituted prima facie evidence of disloyalty to the Stars and Stripes. Nor did the matter of constitutional rights come into question; Japanese ancestry automatically disqualified one from all the rights and privileges of citizenship. Neither was it important that there was not a single instance of espionage or sabotage. A statement by General John L. Dewitt, then head of the Western Defense Command, reveals the confused mentality of a significant segment of the public: "A Jap's a Jap. It makes no difference whether he is an American citizen or not. . . . They are a dangerous element, whether loyal or not."

The mobilization campaign also found advocates in the higher echelons of government. Congressman Rankin of Mississippi, for one, favored "catching every Japanese in America, Alaska, and Hawaii now and putting them in concentration camps, and shipping them back to Asia as soon as possible. . . ." Despite assurances by military experts that a sustained attack was not only unlikely but impossible, civilian heads of the War Department advised the president to take steps to insure the safety of the West Coast from internal or external aggression.

On February 9, 1942, President Roosevelt issued Executive Order No. 9066 authorizing military commanders to remove all Japanese from strategic defense areas. This order was implemented by Congress, executed by the War Department, approved by the Supreme Court, and supported by public opinion. Few people stood up for the Japanese; anyone who dared oppose the federal action not only incurred the epithet "Jap lover" but also became himself suspect.

Designating Washington, Oregon, Idaho, Montana,

California, Nevada, and Utah as key defense areas, General Dewitt gave orders to round up the Japanese in these states. Posters were put up all over the West Coast, addressed to "All Persons of JAPANESE Ancestry," stipulating that "all Japanese persons, both alien and nonalien, will be evacuated from the above designated area by 12:00 o'clock noon, Tuesday, April 7, 1942." (Note that instead of "American citizen," "nonalien" was used.) About 1,000 Japanese in Hawaii and Alaska who were suspected of disloyalty or were influential community leaders were also arrested or interned, but most of the Japanese in Hawaii, where the numbers were so great, and on the East Coast, where they were so few, escaped relocation because total internment was impractical.

In answer to those Japanese Americans who insisted they were loyal to the United States one congressman replied that any "patriotic" Japanese, "if he wants to make his contribution, will submit himself to a concentration camp." As it turned out, this is exactly what happened. Very few Japanese resisted the order for evacuation or bothered to test its constitutionality through legal procedures. For a number of reasons, connected with the norms of the Japanese community, the vast majority meekly submitted to government orders and cooperated completely with the authorities.

Japanese immigrants on the West Coast were not the only ones to bear this unmerited injustice. Reasoning born of ignorance caused Japanese as far away as South America also to be interned in America. In 1942 the United States Department of State arranged for over 2,000 Japanese in South America to be brought to the United States, where they were earmarked as trade bait for American citizens held in countries occupied by Japan. Many were native-born citizens of the South American countries from which they were taken.

When they arrived in the United States, they were placed in internment camps and shifted about from one to another as negotiations for human barter went on. Even when it became obvious that they could not be traded, the Japanese from South America were still held captive. Proceedings after the war were begun to deport them to Japan *for having entered the country without proper papers*. Many did not wish to go to Japan, desiring only to go back to South America. After a long series of legal moves, they won the right to return to Peru, from which most had come, but that country refused their request for reentry. Back in the courts, they won the right to apply for legal residence in the United States and many eventually became citizens.

As part of the opening phase of internment the Japanese on the West Coast, numbering over 117,000, were placed under strict curfew and forced to sell their property at prices that were absurdly low. Some families were lucky enough to entrust their property to reliable friends who promised to hold it for them until after the war. Less fortunate families, however, who could not arrange sales at all, had to abandon their property without compensation. Estimates place the total losses sustained at anywhere between $200 and $400 million, but the final total may have been even higher. After the war the federal government "generously" consented to compensate those families that filed claims of losses, but by 1964, when the last of the claims was settled, the government had authorized only $38 million.

In March 1942, many Japanese families found themselves without the homes and lands they had labored to buy, as penniless as when they first arrived as immigrants, and, far worse, on their way to be interned for no one knew how long. Of the 117,000 Japanese relocated, over 70,000 were American citizens. For this group the question of nationality posed a real dilemma. They were not Japanese subjects, yet the United States government, ignoring the fact of their citizenship, refused to honor their right to be Japanese Americans. No matter the degree of their Americanization, by a twist of physiological irony they were Americans in a cruel disguise.

3

Exiles
in the
Promised Land

IN LATE AUGUST of 1942, under close military surveillance, the Okimoto family filed out of the sequestered compounds of Santa Anita Assembly Center, part of a large group of persons obediently boarding a nonscheduled train ready for a one-way trip to the wilderness of Arizona. After the last passenger stepped in, guards locked the doors and windows and the "Oriental Express" belched out black smoke as it rumbled toward Poston, Arizona, the largest of ten relocation centers scattered in seven states. Behind them the makeshift evacuation center was torn down even more rapidly than it had gone up, and passed into the pages of American history forever a national disgrace.

The trip was long and monotonous; inside the crowded train it was painfully hot. The windows had been sealed tightly to prevent escape. The Okimoto baby, barely two weeks old, had trouble breathing and as the hours dragged on he appeared more dead than alive. Frantic, Kirie hurried through the train until she found a medical unit. They had an oxygen tent, and in this the child passed the remainder of the trip. Anguished thoughts ran through Kirie's mind that perhaps this "mistake" was not destined to live very long. Inside the plastic tent the child cried out incessantly. But the sound of screams growing more and more insistent was welcomed by the mother as a sign that he was still very much alive and that breathing was becoming easier. While in the oxygen tent the child contracted pneumonia, but it at least kept him alive.

Poston was a rude shock to many of the evacuees, whose sensitivities to the nuances of nature had been conditioned by the green hills, verdant valleys, and richly flowering landscape of the West Coast. Poston stood on a sere desert plain through which the Colorado River snakes its way. In the same state that boasts the majesty of the Grand Canyon, Poston could claim little to redeem its existence: it was a wilderness of cactus and sweltering heat where dust storms swirled through at blinding speeds. On moonlit, still nights coyotes howled plaintively in the distance and even sagebrush hurried on through, as if the desolation were too great to endure.

On this flatland a vast area had been enclosed by barbed-wire fence. This was to be the home of most of the large, dispossessed band of Japanese for the duration of the war. The enclosure was divided into three distinct camps, each of which was subdivided into blocks where long, narrow barracks, each roughly one hundred feet by twenty-five, stretched out in neat, orderly lines, separated occasionally by firebreaks. The barracks were partitioned into four sections, each occupied by a family or group. The living quarters, measuring twenty-five by twenty-five feet, were uniformly drab, furnished only with straw mattresses; accessories such as shelves, closets, chairs, tables, and bookcases had to be built by the occupants themselves. The gray, tar-papered buildings within the demarcated zone, watched from lookout posts by green-garbed guards armed with rifles and machine guns, reflected the style of life within them: austere, barren, caged. To call these quarters a relocation center, as the government did, was plainly a euphemism. Internment camp—or if one chooses to be more descriptive, concentration or prisoner-of-war camp— came closer to capturing the essence of what Poston and similar centers represented.

Superficially at least, life within the camps went on as if little were out of the ordinary. There were no mass murders, no Auschwitz-like atrocities, no tortures; nor were there riots, rebellions, or sit-down strikes by the captives except at Tule Lake where people desiring repatriation and loyalty suspects had been placed. Neither was there any real resistance or nihilistic slothfulness; true to ethnic form, a strong sense of community helped the Japanese make the best of a bad situation.

The 20,000 internees at Poston went about their occupations with exemplary orderliness and purpose. Farmers grew food, carpenters repaired buildings, teachers ran classes, and doctors attended the sick. The area within the perimeter of the fences represented a self-sufficient community which for three years was the only world that existed for its inhabitants. It would have been difficult, judging from the prosaic pace of life inside, to suspect that outside the most devastating war in human history was being waged, and that the world of the camp and the world of war were somehow linked.

At Poston the Okimotos threw themselves busily into church work. On weekdays, after sending the older children off to school, they studied the Bible and meditated for the rest of the morning, then called on members of the congregation; on Sundays they conducted church services. Certainly for them internment did not seriously warp the routine of their daily lives or impair the effectiveness of their calling.

Before evacuation the Okimotos had lived in a church parsonage, owning no land and having very few personal belongings; they consequently sustained almost no financial loss by the change. Indeed, they may well have been among those few whose material livelihood actually improved as a result of internment. In San Diego, their home before the war, they collectively earned a salary of around $110 monthly; only careful spending enabled them to feed, clothe, and educate three growing children. In camp the family was fed in the communal dining halls and housed in the barracks. Unpalatable as both food and lodging seemed at times, there was nonetheless no lack of nutrition, and the rent was unbeatable.

Camp life also placed the missionary couple squarely in the midst of those people they had crossed the Pacific to serve. There could not have been a better opportunity to mingle with immigrants and their children; some of the friends made during the three years were among the closest they ever had. In camp they widened immensely their circle of acquaintances, deepened their own understanding of Japanese-American society, and in the process sharpened their effectiveness as ministers.

But even for the Okimotos—whose adjustment to Poston was probably among the least painful—internment still constituted in human and spiritual terms an ugly interlude. The three older children recall only too clearly the bafflement and fear they felt when they were jerked out of their playgrounds, marched onto trains by rifle-bearing soldiers, and interned in the middle of the desert with a colony of Japanese captives. No explanation for the federal action could be given to children in terms that were readily understandable. They could make no sense of the forced separation from their playmates. Nor could their minds grasp the reasoning that said their loyalties were to Japan rather than America. One child had never seen the country and the other two were too young to remember Japan.

Since they had done no wrong, the only way they could possibly interpret internment was to assume that they were being punished for being Japanese. Every Japanese, after all, was supposed to be bad; as they and their parents were Japanese, they too had to be locked up in concentration camps. The result of this assumption was that they grew to despise the Japanese part of themselves and to feel ashamed for being somehow related to a people who would dare strike so underhandedly at Americans. The psychological wounds went deep, leaving permanent scars that caused them to feel apologetic for their ethnicity. They were estranged from the mainstream of American life for some time. Even for the youngest child, spending the first three years of his life behind barbed-wire fences exclusively among his racial kind probably affected not only his basic feelings of trust but also in subtle, subconscious ways shaped what were to become his adult attitudes and whole sense of selfhood.

Even though on the surface activity went on as normal, the emotional substance of the lives of the interned was grotesquely distorted. Everything was rigidly regimented and monotonous: the same buildings, always the familiar surroundings, set hours for meals, regular routines, prescribed procedures, the next day the same as the one before. Daily existence was devoid of the pleasure of surprise; the greatest excitement each day—for some the only thing to look forward to—was mail delivery. A sense of ennui hung oppressively in the air. At times Rev. and Mrs. Okimoto felt envy for the coyotes calling in the distance, for at least they were not caged.

The Japanese in camps lived a life which, despite its material security and apparent normalcy, was fundamentally inhuman. Without freedom the years of confinement were largely wasted, barren, and spiritually brutal. Under these circumstances it is hardly surprising that unforeseen tensions invaded the lives of many inhabitants. The Okimotos' usual pattern of living was radically changed when the entire family was squeezed together in the same small room, separated only by a thin wall from the occupants of the neighboring unit. There everything a family said or did could be overheard and the most important question in life came to be: how much longer would one be trapped in the desert prison. Underlying tensions occasionally erupted into heated quarrels, emotional arguments, and petty bickering over trivia, straining relationships in the usually close Okimoto household.

It was hard for someone as proud as Tameichi to accept the armed patrols, the authoritarian commands, and the sense of helplessness without feeling deeply resentful. It was particularly frustrating that he, who had so firmly rejected Japanese militarism, should be held accountable for it in the United States. The sense of injustice was driven home when the government handed down a loyalty oath which he, like all Japanese over seventeen, either had to sign or face the Tule Lake camp and ultimate deportation. The coercion was humiliating evidence that by virtue of his race he was considered a traitor and a subversive, unless he swore in writing otherwise.

Tameichi managed largely to suppress his feelings at the time. Afterwards he blotted many of the most grating episodes out of his consciousness, seldom bringing the subject of internment up in conversation. But Poston came back to him periodically during sleep. Twenty-five years later Tameichi still would toss violently in his sleep and scream, "Let me out! Let me out of this concentration camp!" or, "We can't let them do this to us. We have our rights and we've got to stand up for them!"

But of the 117,000 Japanese interned, the hardest hit may have been those nisei, numerically two-thirds of the evacuated population, who were in their late adolescence and early adulthood. For them, incarceration meant at best an interruption of their college education and at worst an abrupt termination of it. College was for them not only an opportunity to deepen their understanding of life but also an indispensible means of acquiring specific vocational skills. The internment deprived this group of the freedom to choose its own careers. Many who aspired to better jobs were forced into gardening or garage work.

Most nisei nonetheless begged for a chance to prove their loyalty by serving in the armed forces. The federal government, however, classified all nisei as enemy aliens in June 1942, barring them from military service. The Japanese American Citizens League (JACL) protested this measure and fought vigorously to have it changed. But JACL objections went unheeded until the shortage of manpower for the war became apparent. As the death tolls rose, it was decided finally to bestow upon Japanese Americans the privilege of volunteering for "their country." In a statement that now sounds almost deliberately tongue-in-cheek, President Roosevelt said, "No loyal citizen of the United States should be denied the democratic right to exercise the responsibilities of his citizenship regardless of his ancestry." Spelled out concretely, this generous statement meant that nisei were to have the "democratic right" to die for the United States even if they were deprived of the equally basic right to live normally within its constitutional laws.

The choice put before the twenty-year-old Japanese American was simple: either stay behind barbed wire for an indefinite period of time or go out into the battlefronts to fight for the country that had imprisoned him. Many of the nisei already in the services prior to Pearl Harbor had been hastily moved into innocuous, nonsecurity jobs or summarily discharged and placed in internment camps. Some had even been jailed on suspicion of treason and detained in military prisons on no more evidence than that of ancestry.

When interned nisei asked whether risking their lives would facilitate the release of their families, the government's answer was an unequivocal no. Nevertheless a large number of Japanese Americans volunteered for the army. During the war a total of 25,778 Japanese Americans served: 13,528 from the mainland and 12,240 from Hawaii. On January 20, 1944, with manpower exceedingly low, a draft call went out for all eligible nisei, many of whom were still in concentration camps. Out of those who had been locked up for over two years, only 300 refused to be inducted.

In the army the nisei were segregated in separate units, presumably to avoid problems that might arise in integrated groups. When nisei forces, like the 442nd Infantry Combat Team and the 100th Infantry Battalion, reached the European front, little question remained of their loyalties. Once in action these soldiers joined the ranks of the most decorated in the annals of U.S. military history. Their daring and heriosm are legendary: in the Italian campaign alone the 100th Battalion won more than 1,000 Purple Hearts, 11 Distinguished Service Crosses, 44 Silver Stars, 31 Bronze Stars, and 3 Legion of Merit Ribbons. It took immense violence and wartime valor and a staggering toll of over 9,000 casualties to do it, but the nisei fighters eventually won grudging acknowledgment of their loyalty from even the most hard-bitten racist skeptics.

4

The Compliant Patriots

THERE ARE A NUMBER of Americans today who, looking back on internment, fear it could be used against other minorities in the future, particularly those of different skin color. Some Japanese Americans have been so soured by injustices suffered at the hands of bigots that they no longer can bring themselves to trust white citizens. To this small minority a new "relocation" is not just a vague misgiving; in view of the widespread racism in the U.S., it seems a definite possibility. Yesterday's enemy was Japan; tomorrow's could be Communist China. In such an eventuality, what would be the fate of Chinese citizens in America? Although another internment seems unlikely, an ominous note has been recently struck in J. Edgar Hoover's warning that the Chinese-American community could represent a fertile breeding ground for agents of Communist China; however well-intended the motives behind the issuance of this precautionary statement, it sounds a basic theme of political-racist fear which is alarmingly reminiscent of the times just after Pearl Harbor.

It should be pointed out, however, that of all the minority groups living in the United States at the time of Pearl Harbor, probably no other besides the Japanese could have been so effortlessly interned. What other group would have obeyed the mobilization orders so mutely? What other minority would have bowed to and thanked the armed soldiers who escorted them to the camps instead of resisting the action through angry protests and organized legal maneuvers? The reasons underlying what now seems a strangely submissive response are many. Some derive from accidents of number and geography; others relate to the unique cultural outlook of the Japanese Americans.

Almost all the internees were taken from the West Coast, where the Japanese community numbered slightly over 115,000, a size large enough to frighten its neighbors but unfortunately small enough to be readily massed for internment. Moreover, these Japanese were concentrated in a few population pockets along the West Coast, such as Los Angeles, the Bay Area, and Fresno, and so the logistics of transplantation were relatively simple.

The order for internment found the Japanese in America without many supporters. Few Americans were willing to rally to the defense of a minority connected with a nation that, by surprise attack, had forced the U.S. into World War II. Nor, with the exception of a few reliable organizations like the American Civil Liberties Union, were there any civic groups courageous enough to confront intense prejudice and oppose internment, if not for the Japanese themselves, then for the sake of liberty and justice. Other ethnic minorities, preoccupied with their own problems, were also silent.

Neither were there popular Japanese figures of the stature, say, of a Joe DiMaggio or a Joe Louis, around whom effective protest could be organized. Even if there had been, it is questionable whether the ultimate outcome would have been substantially different, for Japan was a feared enemy, a potential victor in all its territorial ambitions in the Pacific, a threat not only to the security of the West Coast, but to the very existence of America. In the panic and patriotic din of the time the Japanese in America suffered the further disadvantage of having lived and worked quietly, avoiding extensive social contacts with those outside the ethnic community, preferring out of shyness to keep unobtrusively to their kind. Their lives passed daily without fanfare until attention was abruptly focused on them that infamous Sunday morning. Because the Japanese were a relatively unknown quantity, their public image could be twisted to confirm widely held suspicions and fears.

This comparative anonymity was a great disadvantage against the strong currents of latent prejudice which had long preceded America's involvement in the war. The anti-Oriental racism that had been turned against the Japanese at the beginning of the century was revived after Pearl Harbor. Seen in this context, it was no accident that those who traced their ancestry to Germany and Italy, with which the United States was also at war, passed through the period uninterned and comparatively unmolested. The Japanese misfortune was their inability to pass physically as "typical" Americans. They were Orientals, and so more suspect, more alien than European immigrants.

The Japanese-American reaction was further complicated by values and traditions brought from Japan and kept alive by issei. Perhaps the most important of these was that authority and group obligations took precedence over the notion of personal rights. Issei certainly, but also many nisei, reared in families where this idea was taken for granted, could not fully appreciate the outrage of having their freedom suddenly stripped away.

In prewar Japan few liberal thinkers, still less the general public, understood or advocated a doctrine of natural rights. Several well-known liberals in the prewar period, such as Hiroyuki Kato and Tetsuro Watsuji, became apostates from the cause of democracy and advocates of a rigid statism, in large part because they could not accept the notion of inherent human rights. Significantly, those men who remained consistent champions of democracy were precisely those who adhered to this notion. The famous Yukichi Fukuzawa, founder of Keio University, and Emori Ueki, one of Meiji Japan's most brilliant political thinkers, were two such individuals.

Accustomed as the Japanese were to thinking in terms of *giri* (obligation, gratitude) and *gimu* (duty, responsibility), two concepts of overriding importance in their lifeview, other notions like human rights were considered secondary. This is not too surprising, for society in Japan was characterized by a high degree of homogeneity and a strong sense of community. The individual and his personal rights were of secondary importance. Given this, most immigrants to America had difficulty grasping the fundamentally different nature and premises of a democratic society. Consequently they did not regard incarceration as such a shocking violation of certain basic rights. In fact, so alien was this idea that some Japanese Americans considered internment an understandable consequence of the war

between Japan and America. A sense of group responsibility, moreover, led many to share a collective sense of
shame for Pearl Harbor even though they themselves had
absolutely nothing to do with it. After release from the
camps, group sensitivity drove them to make bright the
image of the Japanese which had been badly tarnished as
a result of the war. It is doubtful that many young nisei
today would allow themselves to be punished on the basis
of guilt by association. We are aware of our rights and
would fight vigorously to protect them.

The issei carried yet another belief that ill-fitted them to
resist imprisonment: an enormous respect for authority.
When the evacuation order was promulgated, many were
impressed because it carried the full approval of the august
White House. That the *erai* (great, revered) President
Roosevelt had issued the order made it almost unthinkable
to defy. Centuries of submission within an elaborate hierarchy of authority lay behind this reaction.

Equally influential was the belief that *ummei* (fate) determined much of man's life. In Japan, where man is so often
at the mercy of nature's whims in the forms of earthquakes,
floods, and typhoons, belief in an uncontrollable destiny
is not inconsistent. Ummei played its part in the resignation
many felt toward the militarism of the late thirties. Even
today there is in Japan a less pronounced but similar fatalis-
tic acceptance of what the government does. At the time of
internment, many felt that they were caught in a web of
circumstances beyond their control; fate had brought
them to America, and fate was now decreeing that their
lives be uncertain for a time. Consequently, they hunched
their shoulders and thought, *"Shikata ga nai"* (Nothing can
be done about it). Some even tried to look at the brighter

side of confinement, consoling themselves with the thought that forcible deportation or even execution would have been far worse.

A Japanese was not only expected to personify the Confucian principles of obligation, duty, and respect for authority but he was also supposed to practice *enryo* (reserve, restraint) and *gaman* (patience, perseverance). Enryo stresses the need to suppress self-will in the presence of others and often makes a Japanese seem humble and self-effacing. Gaman calls for patience in the face of provocations or crises. Translated into daily behavior, the first means that a man will impose his will upon others or bother them with personal matters only with the greatest reluctance. The second is seen in the almost Promethean forbearance with which the Japanese suffer in silence rather than release pent-up emotions. Many Japanese in America demonstrated both these qualities by quietly obeying evacuation orders and loss of property, by the equanimity with which they bore the screaming monotony of camp life, and in their ability to absorb uncomplainingly sporadic harsh treatment after the war.

The peculiar characteristics of the Japanese ethnic community led, on the one hand, to nonresistance in the face of an authoritarian decree, but, on the other, they prepared the Japanese to make the tough transition to American society, overcoming imposing obstacles of cultural unfamiliarity, language handicap, and racial discrimination. In Japan these traits, combined with other factors, led to the thrusting aside of democracy as well as to the amazing technological modernization of an underdeveloped nation. The nisei, heirs of Japan and of America, produced an amalgamated set of values and attitudes that often provided them with the ability to adapt to American society and indeed to succeed in ways that no other racial minority as yet has.

While the fruits of adversity have proven to be unexpectedly sweet, the fact of internment remains, and men and women who live today are haunted by it. There is much in the episode that is shocking, incredible, and tragic. Looking back, it seems absolutely inexcusable, an unwarranted persecution of an innocent minority and an act of injustice that brought into question some of America's most treasured ideals. At this distance, all the participants seem to share the guilt—the racist agitators, the fence-sitting majority, the mass media, the pressure organizations, the military supervisors, the civilian government, and, paradoxically, even the Japanese who assented to the outrage with barely a whimper. Out of it everyone emerged in some way degraded.

But those Japanese Americans who were the real victims of the event for the most part neither dwell morbidly on what happened nor bear antipathy toward those who treated them as criminals. Perhaps they should feel more outraged, for many underwent personal sufferings to which no human should be subjected. Some returned to Japan, their dreams exploded, their hard work negated, their vigor and will broken. Those who stayed had to face the consequences of financial ruin, prolonged separation from loved ones, and the unmeasurable damage caused by dismal years within deadening detention enclosures.

Yet, as with other seeming disasters in history, a curious force operated to bring life from death, hope from despair, freedom from bondage. Poston and other camps symbolized the close of an uncertain era and the dawn of a new and happier one for all Japanese Americans. "Barely more than twenty years after the end of the wartime camps," writes William Petersen, "this is a minority that has risen above even prejudiced criticism. By any criterion of good citizenship that we choose, the Japanese Americans are better than any other group in our society, including native-born whites. They have established this remarkable record, moreover, by their own almost totally unaided effort. Every attempt to hamper their progress resulted only in enhancing their determination to succeed. Even in a country whose patron saint is the Horatio Alger hero, there is no parallel to this success story."*

In 1960, just fifteen years after the war's end, the median years of education for Japanese Americans was 12.2, as compared to 11.1 for Chinese, 11.0 for whites, 9.2 for Filipinos, and 8.6 for blacks. At the same time those who worked as laborers had fallen from 25 percent in 1940 to 5 percent, while those in the professions had risen from 3.8 percent to 15 percent, roughly the same as for the white majority. In terms of income the Japanese Americans were far ahead of other minorities, while their crime and divorce rates were among the lowest in the country. However serious the damage incurred, it is evident that internment did not permanently cripple the Japanese-American community as a whole.

It can in fact be argued that the best in the internees came out after confinement. Imprisonment seems to have toughened Japanese Americans while reinforcing their determination to do well in life. Older nisei in particular were going to prove, as many did in the 442nd, that they were not only first-class citizens but also eminently capable

*New York Times Magazine, January 9, 1966.

of achieving the highest goals. As a result Japanese Americans gained for themselves that measure of respect they doggedly pursued.

Aside from material gains, there are two other results of internment that mitigate somewhat its bleakness. One is that the pattern of living established by the first wave of immigrants, revolving around rural occupations, was broken. After the war many issei returned to farming, the only work they knew, but a number of nisei moved into occupations which committed them to an urban way of life and provided footholds for upward social mobility.

At the same time the guilt and regret felt by many at the maltreatment of America's Japanese during the war led to the elimination of a great deal of overt discrimination and to the opening (though not fully) of doors once closed to them. Government officials admitted the injustice of internment; prewar legal restrictions on owning land and acquiring citizenship were abolished; wider employment opportunities were made available. Once the way was open and major barriers came down, the Japanese could earn proper rewards for their abilities, and could justly claim to have forged a place for themselves within American society as a whole.

Now a moment in history many have forgotten or would prefer to forget, the internment of Japanese Americans should be remembered for its relevance to present-day problems. Although the episode pained America's conscience sufficiently to lift most barriers against nisei, the formula "Herd 'em up, pack 'em off, and give them the inside room in the badlands," is for many still a valid solution to complex racial problems. This raises the disturbing question of whether the conscience of the American public has to be made to feel guilty before the problems of injustice can be dealt with intelligently. The mute and submissive response of the wartime Japanese to imprisonment was an unusual concurrence of particular circumstances, timing, and cultural outlooks—all of which have changed permanently since that time. The prospect that new acts of brutal repression must occur before Americans will concede to all minorities their full rights and freedoms is particularly unnerving in this, a time of volatile minority unrest.

5

Ghetto, California Style

ONE LATE JANUARY afternoon in 1945, as the wintry Arizona sun slowly drew the crimson sky into the earth, the long-awaited news reached us: internment camps were to be closed during the year. The twilight of imprisonment had come at last to Poston, as to other camps, and everyone expectantly awaited the day of liberation.

The news was greeted by my brothers and sister with jubilation, though my father, by contrast, was more reserved. His somewhat wary mind began immediately to probe the nooks and crannies of implications that eluded the children. He realized that liberation would entail packing again, moving, and resettling in San Diego where he would resume his ministry. It would involve saying goodbye to many close friends, some of whom he might never see again, leaving the security of life among fellow Japanese, and plunging into an unknown existence among non-Japanese who might not welcome the return of "enemy

44

aliens." Yet, the end of internment would also bring release from the barren confines of the desert, the opportunity to roam through the wide-open countryside, and the chance to get back into the stream of activities in the outside world. For his children it would mean attending regular schools and carrying on a normal childhood. The government's decision to disband the camps, in short, meant *freedom*. At last. Regardless of the uncertainties in making the transition, it was exhilarating to think that he and his family would again soon be their own masters.

In June my family began to make the round of farewells. It was a sad, happy moment. I said goodbye to my three- and four-year-old playmates, not realizing I would never see most of them again. My brothers and sister exchanged vague addresses with their friends and made solemn promises to stay in touch. Gathering our things together, we boarded a train once again and pulled out of Poston, headed for San Diego. The long rows of barracks, so gray and tedious during internment, seemed strangely warm and lovable now that they were being left behind forever.

We departed from Poston with no illusions about potential troubles awaiting in California. My father warned repeatedly that we should be prepared to endure the worst possible treatment until the war ended and memories of it died. Many of those released in the winter had met with a cold, often hostile reception. Insults were common; incidents of terrorism occurred here and there: houses put aflame, dynamite set off, threats of physical harm made, and shots fired by vigilante groups. As the war neared its end, however, the antagonisms of the West Coast population gradually diminished, and most Japanese could move about free from fear of physical injury.

In August atomic bombs were dropped on Hiroshima and Nagasaki. Since many issei had immigrated from Hiroshima, there was widespread concern over the safety of relatives and friends. In the same week Russia declared war on Japan, and many began to fear that if Japan did not surrender soon the whole nation would be obliterated. Capitulation, most Japanese Americans thought, was merely a matter of time.

The end came, mercifully, not long after the A-bomb blast at Hiroshima, on August 14, 1945, when the Japanese cabinet officially accepted the terms of unconditional surrender. The day coincidentally was my third birthday, the first celebrated in the big, varied outside world I had never seen before. During the first three years of my life, passed behind barbed fences in the desert, an old militaristic Japan had died convulsively and a new peaceful nation was about to emerge. August 14, 1945 was not only the birthday of my own freedom and a fresh new start on life, but the beginning of a new Japan rising from the ashes and colossal tragedy of world war. Like most Japanese in America, my parents welcomed the news, glad for the Allied victory, anguished over the suffering in Japan, but delighted that life could be normal again.

When my family returned to San Diego, they found the city they once knew altered. The neighborhood where my father's church was located had been the home of a number of Japanese before internment. Even before the war this area, compared with other parts of the city, had been a rundown, substandard housing district where many races mixed, including Negroes, Mexicans, and Japanese. After the Japanese were evacuated, their homes were taken over by Negro families which had moved from the rural South in search of better employment opportunities. With the heavy influx of Negroes and the northward migration of Mexicans, the district had become a ghetto, inhabited predominantly by poverty-blighted Negroes who had neither the means nor the liberty to move into more comfortable neighborhoods.

Though bad, San Diego's ghetto was not nearly as grim as the tenements of New York City's Harlem. It more resembled Watts in Los Angeles, with its straight lines of small, shabby houses; unkempt lawns; broken-down garages; corner drugstores that displayed racks of obscene magazines; small, fly-infested grocery stores; and gas stations with dirty smelly toilets, on the walls of which were scribbled pithy profanities. There were dank little bars where men with glazed faces stood hunched over the counters and dreary dance halls in front of which fat old lipstick-smeared madams sat calling out in husky voices to passersby while swatting with their fans at the mosquitos and moths circling overhead. On Saturday nights pink Cadillacs pulled up to the bars and cool black men in shiny sharkskin suits could be seen sauntering slowly down the streets against a background of honky-tonk sounds of the barroom jukeboxes, the sounds broken now and then by the high-pitched, raucous laughter of drunken women. There was none of the fearful, underlying violence of Harlem. But San Diego's ghetto was drab, dreary, despairing, a dead end for many of its inhabitants.

The prewar parsonage, now more weather beaten, stood in the middle of this ghetto. It was a small, old house, very much like the others on the block, originally painted white but by 1945 a dirty, peeling gray with two creaky screen doors. My family's livelihood was below that of most Negroes in the neighborhood. On the $140-a-month salary my father received from his tiny congregation we all had to subsist. Naturally, our food wasn't exactly the kind gourmets thrive on; yet like many issei sticklers about health, my parents stretched our food budget as far as possible to include balanced meals of high nutritional content. Usually we mixed simple Japanese and Western dishes in the same meal. Rice was served every day for dinner and occasionally for lunch, with the main course varying according to what was on sale at the local food store.

Our Negro friends were always a bit astonished to see us eating raw tuna, dried seaweed, raw eggs, and fermented soy beans—and not with forks and spoons, but with chopsticks. In place of candy, we ate dried squid, a common snack in Japan. It was not a very appetizing substitute for Baby Ruth bars, but it was all we got. I looked forward to going with my parents to the homes of Japanese friends because of the many treats offered. It was the custom among issei to lavish fine food on visitors, even if it sometimes required going beyond one's means to do so.

Poor as we were, there was little danger of starving so long as we were part of the Japanese-American community. The Japanese in America, especially after the war, retained a binding sense of community, which knitted all together into what was almost an extended family, close and interdependent. Watching out for the well-being of their own people, the Japanese gave generously of their time and possessions to help needy families like ours. On those occasions when my mother could scrape the food barrel no lower, and we would wonder where our next meal would come from, there would often be a knock heard at our door. On the porch—with no one in sight—bags of groceries and sometimes steaming hot meals would be left. She was convinced it was the work of God; if so, the agents of delivery were undoubtedly big-hearted Japanese friends who knew of our plight and did not want to embarrass us with what might be regarded as handouts or charitable offerings. The kind of emotional and physical security we found in the Japanese-American community helped us immeasurably in making the transition to the outside world.

We had come to San Diego expecting to face a chilly, antagonistic atmosphere, and the reception received was not exactly friendly. My family, like most Japanese-American families all over the West Coast, met with its share of animosity from Negroes, Mexicans, and whites. It was perhaps unavoidable, given the almost insane hatred for "Japs" that had been drummed up during the war, to encounter intense hostility right after Japan's surrender. My brothers and sister were called names and chased around at times by school bullies, but their problems were mild in comparison with those of Japanese Americans in other neighborhoods, who often had to band together to defend themselves against physical assault. To protect themselves from gang beatings, some nisei were forced to swear they were Chinese, not Japanese. But in general, most were able to deal with aggression, both because they had been prepared for it and because they wanted anxiously to be accepted by society. My parents drilled into us the importance of beating prejudice not by fighting all those who provoked us, but by showing them that we, as nisei, could do as well or better than they in all fields of endeavor. The fastest, most effective way to be accepted, they reminded us, was to win the respect of non-Japanese through fair competition.

Like almost all nisei children we were taught early that education and industry were the indispensable passports to social success; without them we could go nowhere in life. My parents were vitally interested in our academic progress, punishing us for indolence or failure to excel, encouraging us for bringing back straight-A report cards. In spite of our poverty, my father's library was always packed with books; he was an insatiable reader who would spend nearly all of his spare time voraciously consuming works in English, Japanese, Greek, and Hebrew. Friends of the family learned never to give him money for his birthday because, even though he wore tattered clothes, he invariably spent it on second-hand books. By my parent's dispensation of rewards and punishments, as well as by example, we were made to understand that on our performance at school rested not only our own futures but the hopes and expectations of our parents; it was almost as if the sum worth of their immigrant lives hinged upon how successfully we performed. There was therefore never any question about whether we were headed for college or not, for a life without a college diploma was as unimaginable as dinner without chopsticks and rice.

To obtain admission to the best possible colleges—that is, the ones with the most prestige and the most advantageous routes to social prominence—called for unstinting industry and the application of all our energies. If getting better marks at school required working twice as hard as our classmates, then that was the price that had to be paid. My parents, who had been brought up in Japan to esteem hard work and scorn laziness, found confirmation of these values in their Calvinistic brand of Christianity and became unshakable believers in the Horatio Alger-type creeds of social success. "America is a land of opportunity," my father was fond of telling us. "Unlike Japan, where you are what you are born, in America anyone, even a humble, self-educated farmer like Abraham Lincoln, can become president."

When I asked whether a Japanese American could ever become president someday, he always assured me that through education and diligence anything was possible in the United States. If I applied myself, he said, I could become America's first nisei president. The supreme confidence with which he offered these assurances was quite astounding since we had only just been released from the internment camp. It was a testament not only to the intensity of his faith in the efficacy of the American way of life, but to his naïveté concerning the magnitude of racial discrimination in America.

6

Yellow, Black, White

I RECALL THOSE DAYS in San Diego, my introduction to the world outside Poston, with great nostalgia. I doubt, however, if my family could live today in a ghetto. The whole mood of black people has changed so drastically that Japanese families would no longer find themselves welcomed in ghetto areas. In a span of twenty-five years the blacks have changed from passive acceptance of the status quo to militant assertion of black power, from quiet tolerance of myths about inferiority to aggressive declarations of racial and cultural pride, from Ralph Bunche and Jackie Robinson to Eldridge Cleaver and Muhammad Ali. What is taking place is nothing less than a revolution. And having seen the conditions under which blacks have been forced to live, the only question in my mind is not why they are revolting so passionately but why they waited so long to do so.

The accumulated rage and verbal virulence of some of the more militant black groups have frightened and per-

52

plexed many people. Some of those disquieted by the fiery rhetoric have asked me: "Why do the blacks talk so violently? Why do they complain, provoke, and riot? Why can't they be more like you Japanese Americans? You never caused any trouble even when interned. You never complained to the federal government nor used foul-mouthed language nor acted lawlessly. You're a model minority, and race relations would be far better if all minorities behaved like you people."

I wince when such comments are made because they grossly oversimplify problems. This viewpoint, however sincerely expressed, is first of all an insult to blacks as well as to Japanese Americans. It is based upon the subtle but baleful misconception that freedom and equality have to be earned from the white community that sits in judgment, dispensing justice magnanimously when it so pleases, and that these privileges are not God-given, *inalienable rights,* as eloquently stated by the founders of the United States. It moreover makes no allowances for the obstacles standing in the way of Negroes that never impeded the Japanese, such as a history of enslavement. If some blacks sound extreme today it is because they suffered from oppression long before the Japanese ever reached the American continent and because, even while the Japanese have largely won their rights, the blacks are still waiting and are reaching the end of their patience.

Furthermore this view is superficial insofar as it ignores the uniqueness of the Japanese-American story. That the ethnic heritage of the Japanese people happened to coincide nicely with certain important values—like hard work, frugality, achievement—which were so integral a part of the Protestant tradition in America was a stroke of good fortune for us. Not all ethnic legacies blend so readily with the culture of an adopted country; it is wrong always to expect such happy marriages.

Two other factors must also be considered which make our experience different from that of the blacks. Whereas the black population is twenty-two-odd million, ours does not even come to half a million; obviously it is easier to accommodate a smaller minority population for the simple reason that it involves fewer social dislocations. The blacks also suffer greater penalties as a consequence of physical characteristics that depart radically from white standards of beauty.

Nor must it be overlooked that the successes of Japanese Americans have come at a price of rigid conformity to white middle-class standards of success and respectability. We were accepted in large measure because we fitted white modes of behavior; we abided by the laws, entertained few thoughts of revolution or reform, worked hard within the extant social framework, bore prejudice mutely, and generally pleased the white community with our self-effacing, deferential attitudes. Those who wish to interpret our behavior in a favorable light call it "adaptability." Others might with equal justification describe it as "kowtowing." At any rate the Japanese Americans represented no threat to the status quo, and accommodation of the 474,000 Japanese was able to proceed without major social changes.

In one sense it can be argued that the pattern of Japanese conformity basically failed to produce permanent social reforms that might have corrected the sickness of racial prejudice in society—prejudice was simply focused more sharply on other racial groups. The civil rights movement, despite its traumas and complications and halting progress, if positively resolved will have a much greater impact on American society in terms of battering down the walls of discrimination and effecting badly needed reforms in the structure of the social order than the inroads we have been able to make. This is not to denigrate our achievement; it is simply to put it into historical perspective and to stress that our way of doing things was by no means necessarily the only or best one. If the present racial crisis can be successfully lived through, the black movement will perhaps go down as the greatest social crusade in twentieth-century American history, beside which the Japanese-American story will seem almost inconsequential.

The nisei road to social acceptance has exacted a high toll in terms of loss of ancestral identity, sacrifice of creativity, intolerance toward nonconformity, and adherence to the security of the Japanese-American subculture. This aspect of the upward social course plotted by Japanese Americans must not be overlooked in any assessment of our loudly trumpeted success story, particularly in view of the present search for ancestral roots among the blacks and the blossoming of creative impulses among black writers.

Finally, it must be pointed out that perhaps the single most decisive factor in the divergent nisei and Negro paths to success has been the differences of opportunities and expectations between the two racial groups. For Japanese Americans opportunities are simply much greater than they are for blacks; it is natural therefore that we have had higher expectations and aspirations. There can be no denying that we could never have reached our present position of prosperity without a radical opening up of opportunities. No amount of industry, no quantity of frugality, nor any abundance of perseverance could have brought us where we are. Without openings we would have been battering our heads against a stone wall and ending up as frustrated and perhaps as enraged as black Americans are today.

For these reasons it can be seriously questioned whether our particular road to success can be followed or if indeed it is worth following. True, we are probably a quaint model for conservatives who can conveniently point to us and say, "Why can't the others be like you?" Consistent with our pattern, many of us would probably respond with a smile of pride, modestly replying, "What we did was really nothing." In fact that reply would be accurate, for in some vital respects we have done nothing: on our way up the social ladder we have caused no trouble, stirred up no controversy, and made no permanent alterations of an essentially racist status quo. Although we have won the material spoils of victory in our own struggle against discrimination, we have done little to lighten the burden of other minorities, for whom the battle still lies largely ahead.

As one who has lived among blacks, I find it easy to understand why they, after laboring in the ghettos and cotton fields one hundred years overtime, have produced dedicated militants, boiling with rage, determined to win justice for their people, and convinced of the need for violence to achieve their objectives. Although I cannot always agree with the programs and methods of such organizations as the Black Panthers, since their tactics seem to be counterproductive in the long run to the black cause, I can certainly sympathize with their emotional fury when every day they are demeaned in countless ways as human beings and are caught in a vicious self-perpetuating cycle of stagnancy in the ghettos.

The lofty image of America as the great land of equality and boundless opportunity appears to be a myth which, though not harmful as an ideal, clouds distinctions between fact and fiction. It has been used to lull people into believing America is an egalitarian society as well as to shift the weight of blame for inequalities on the alleged indolence and ignorance of the very people who suffer most. America is by no means the only country in the world where injustices exist, to be sure, but probably in no other nation is the gap between the ideal and the real so enormous. That the American gift for fantasy and self-delusion is unmatched is shown in the large number of faithful who continue to insist that the American Dream *is* reality—even though many of those whose misfortune it was to be born into a racial minority are swearing that nothing could be farther from the truth. The speed with which racial antagonisms will be settled in America could depend on the rapidity with which those who view the U.S. as a golden melting pot open their eyes to the ugly truth: American society, as it now exists, is deeply racist. This is a fact which is unpleasantly clear to me even as a member of the Japanese-American minority, one of the most fully accepted groups in the postwar period. I can imagine how the blacks and Mexicans and Puerto Ricans must feel about the vaunted American Dream; for them it is no doubt more a nightmare.

The racial tensions that face America today constitute one of the nation's most urgent problems; if solutions to the crisis are not soon found the volatile situation could explode, dooming the country to a divisiveness no amount of time or effort will heal. As seen recently in urban and campus confrontations, black Americans are no longer content with tokenism. They will not sit around another hundred years waiting for the rest of the nation to grant reluctantly what is already guaranteed them under the Constitution. They are surfeited with fraudulent promises, hypocritical arguments, and grudging concessions. Like all racial minorities, the blacks want nothing less than full justice and equality. And they want it now.

The onus of effort is on the shoulders of the white majority. Those holding power must open up the middle and top levels of society to able members of minorities who have been blocked from advancement either by disadvantages of background or by outright discrimination. Complete understanding between whites and nonwhites may still be a distant goal, but reduction of tensions and concrete steps in the direction of harmonious racial coexistence, beginning with knocking down barriers to socio-economic opportunities, can and should be the goals of all the American peoples.

In this endeavor it is my hope that the Japanese-American community will assume an active role. The attitude that equality for yellow is all right, but not for black or brown, still exists in many quarters today. It is up to all Japanese Americans to see that such forms of selected prejudice are not permitted. Although in the postwar period the nisei community has been one of the few minority groups to share for the most part in the opportunities and privileges enjoyed by the majority, we must not be deluded into believing that our work is done. Discrimination in any form, whatever racial minority it is directed against, is an enemy of all; it can easily be turned against anyone of us. Hence, involving ourselves in the continuing fight against injustice is not only a moral but also a practical imperative. To ignore the pleas for help from other minority groups is to participate in the type of racial bigotry that was directed so ruthlessly against Japanese Americans; to participate even passively in discrimination is to forget entirely the experience of internment.

7

The Japanese-American Legend

AS LEGEND WOULD have it, the struggle of the Japanese-American people against racial oppression is a drama that comes to a convulsive climax in the dark hours of internment; after this crisis the nation repents of its injustices and the postwar story of this minority suddenly becomes a happy, heart-warming epilogue of complete assimilation and conquest over prejudice. This happy tale of success suggests that all the prewar suffering was merely a transitional period, a brief, unavoidable prelude to the ultimate eradication of anti-Japanese discrimination in all its brutal forms. The unfortunate consequence of this myth, however, is that the outrages of the past tend to be forgotten, if not excused entirely, and the evidences of lingering prejudice overlooked. Those who subscribe to this myth tend to be so dazzled by the vast improvement in the postwar treatment of Japanese Americans that they are blinded to the racial hostilities that continue to simmer in society.

The prewar tribulations of our race is no valid starting point for comparison; it must not be regarded as a harsh conditioning period against which our postwar gains are properly measured. It is my opinion, based upon some bitter personal experiences, that the undeniable amelioration of the atmosphere after the war is an indication of just how intolerable the prewar situation was, not proof that prejudice in the postwar period has been eliminated. Long after our release from internment my family and I have been stung by racist antagonisms with sufficient regularity to view legends of full assimilation skeptically.

My family's efforts to locate a home in Pasadena, a middle-class residential area just east of Los Angeles, is typical of the kind of unspoken but pernicious discrimination that can still confront Americans of Japanese descent. In 1954, after we had decided to move to Pasadena, my parents set about in search of a home suited to the size of both our family and budget—not an easy order, given the largeness of our needs and the paucity of our resources. They found one that roughly fitted their specifications, but because the white neighbors made it known that Japanese would not be welcomed, they were forced to continue the search elsewhere. After further leg work they discovered another house that met their needs. But again they were thwarted by white neighbors who protested vociferously against "Japs" devaluing the property in their neighborhood. Again my parents accepted the protests and moved on, not wanting to provoke undue trouble, as is characteristic of many issei couples, if an alternative solution could be found.

Finally they discovered a modest house that under the circumstances seemed as nice as they could expect. But once more they were confronted with a barrage of complaints from white neighbors who, invoking the same arguments used against blacks, claimed that if one Jap family moved in, hordes of them would soon descend on the district. Ironically, the residents who voiced this fear were all associated in one way or another with a fundamentalist Christian church which unashamedly preaches love of all races. The fact that my parents were both ministers apparently mattered less to them than the obvious fact that they were Orientals.

With the disparity between felicitous words and ugly reality so apparent in the attitudes of fellow Christians, my parents' mood shifted away from an inclination to accommodate to others' wishes. They came slowly to realize on this, the third encounter with discrimination, that if they allowed their Japanese instincts to dictate their own attitudes, they might well be forced to look vainly for years before finding an area where they would be happily accepted. At the urging of the children, who were much more indignant about the refusals than they were, my parents finally took a decisive stand. After consulting with our nisei realtor, they agreed that continued acquiescence to prejudicial pressures was out of the question. They saw a house; they wanted it; they knew they could raise the money to buy it. It did not seem fair to them that a group of neighbors could interfere in their business transaction without violating their legal rights as naturalized citizens. Consequently, they were determined to resist any action that threatened to compromise their prerogative to purchase the house and if this stand led to legal squabblings, so be it; they were in no mood to be intimidated. In the face of this adamant attitude the neighbors resigned themselves to the idea of having Japanese in the area, probably hoping and praying that no other Orientals—or worse yet from their perspective, Negroes—would follow in our footsteps.

The day we moved into Pasadena will always stand out sharply in my memory because of the ridicule to which I was subjected in entering an upper-middle-class, solidly white junior high school. On the day school started, I rose early in our new home, washed, and put on my best clothes for school: a pair of Levis whose original dark hue had been washed almost white, a checkered Scotch plaid shirt handed down from my brothers, and a new pair of tennis shoes. After registering as one of only two Japanese Americans in the whole school, I made my way with the help of a map to my first-period class, English Composition. Although I lost my way once, I was finally able to locate the room. I stood there a minute, slightly out of breath, my palms sweating in nervousness. Summoning my courage, I took hold of the cold door handle and, pulling back, walked boldly into the classroom. The teacher, who had been lecturing in front, turned my way and stopped talking; the thirty-five students in the classroom turned their heads in my direction. Suddenly silence. For five or six seconds the awful silence persisted. It was deafening.

Why are they staring at me like that? I wondered. A paralysis rooted me to the spot. Don't they realize it's rude to stare? What's the matter? Haven't they ever seen a Japanese American before? I know I'm not as smartly dressed as they are and I'm not a typical blue-eyed blonde. But my eyes and skin aren't that different and my clothes aren't that funny. What's going on? Why don't they stop gaping!

I did not know what to do. I just stood there dumbly.

Then, from the front of the room rose one horselike whinny that suddenly soared into a terrible roar that ricocheted around the ceiling. I looked quickly over at the boy who started the laughter. His head was thrown back and he was shaking convulsively. I looked next at a lovely blonde girl, whose light blue eyes were nearly closed with laughter. Others in the room held their stomachs or pointed at me and looked at each other while riding the momentum of the guffaw. Never in my life had I felt so humiliated. I quickly looked down at the floor, afraid of bursting into tears. I bit my lips and tried to survive the insult without losing my composure. Tears collected around my eyes as the roar continued, but I fought them off, not wanting to give the class the pleasure of seeing me cry.

Staring down at the floor I kept hoping the laughter would soon stop. But it did not. I wanted to crawl into some hole and hide. With my head hung in utter humiliation I asked myself what crime I had committed to be subjected to such cruel treatment. They didn't know me. I was new. I had simply walked in. What possessed them to taunt me like this? My shirt? My old Levis? Could it really be because I was Japanese?

I wanted to know the answer. I looked up again, only to find their laughing, mocking faces unchanged. In desperation, I looked to the teacher for help. Why doesn't he make them stop? It's his responsibility to keep order in the room. But when I found his face it too was contorted in laughter. I felt helpless. Stripped of all dignity I stood there like a dumb, sad-faced clown, clutching with all my might at my scratched lunch pail. God, why did we ever move to Pasadena? I thought. Why didn't someone warn me about this? What right do these rich white kids have to make me feel like some kind of baboon? Who do they think they are?

I looked up again, this time with anger and accusation in my heart. I saw the boy in the front row still snickering. And the pretty blue-eyed girl holding one hand over her open mouth. And the rest of them still savoring the assassination of my soul and whole sense of being. I watched and I hated them. I vowed to myself in that moment that before I graduated from high school they would—all of them— treat me with respect. Whatever the cost, I would pay it. I was going to prove to them that I was not only as good as they were, but better. "Damn rich white kids! Wearing your shiny new Ivy League pants with the fancy buckles on the back," I said to myself. "Enjoy your laugh while you can. You'll never laugh at me again."

When the room quieted down the teacher spoke up: "What's your name, young man?"

"Daniel Okimoto," I replied, almost whispering.

"What? Speak up, young man. I can't hear you."

"Daniel Okimoto," I said louder, my voice quivering. At the sound of my name the whole room broke into convulsed laughter again.

"Hey," said the boy in the front row to the blonde girl next to him. "Did you hear that? Daniel—get that—Daniel Locomoto."

"Locomoto," echoed some others in the class. "Locomotive." "Loco." "Hey, that's Loco over there." "Cocomoto." "Coconut." "Yoo-hoo, Coconut Head," jeered one as he began scratching his armpits in imitation of a monkey.

"Hey, kid," said one of the class tough boys. "Is that a Chinaman's name or a Jap's name? Are you a yellow-bellied Chinaman or a sneaky, dirty Jap?"

Fortunately the teacher quieted them down this time before the teasing got any further out of hand. I glared over at the boy who had just called me a sneaky, dirty Jap, suppressing a strong urge to spit on him. "You'll get yours, buster," I thought. "I'm willing to take you on, right here. You and that donkey sitting in the first row; both of you, together."

"All right, Daniel," instructed the teacher, "your seat is right over there."

I took my seat, relieved to leave the front of the room. The teacher resumed the English Composition lesson. I began taking notes, even though I was still flushed with anger and could not concentrate. A few minutes later something hit me squarely in the face. A spitball lay beside me; a few aisles away a couple of boys were snickering. I decided to ignore them and started writing again. Suddenly a hand swung around from the boy in front and knocked me in the head. I sat there furious. While I was debating whether to punch him or not, I felt my ears being pulled hard from behind. I turned around and saw a girl looking innocently up at the ceiling. Girl or not, I was tempted to swing at her. Then began the whispered barbs: "I wonder if the Jap boy can speak English," sneered one boy, thinning his eyes out grotesquely to caricature Orientals. "Honorable Jap boy, you speak English?"

When the class finally ended, I rushed to my next classroom in order to avoid a repetition of the same experience. I got there before anyone else and chose a seat situated as inconspicuously in the back of the room as possible. Soon the rest of the class came marching in, chattering away familiarly. One boy, with a pencil stuck behind his ear, took a seat next to mine. When he noticed me, he asked the girl in front, "Who's the idiot sitting behind you?" I said nothing. The boy stared at me for a few long minutes, then spoke. "Kid, are you a Jap or a Chinaman?" Not wanting to dignify his question with an answer, I ignored him completely. The boy kept up his taunting. "Hey, you."

"Are you speaking to me?" I asked.

"Yeah, who do you think I'm talking to, your desk?"

"I have a name. If you want to talk to me, use it."

"What is it? Little Jappy Boy? Charlie Chan? Mr. Moto?"

I kept quiet even though my eyes must have betrayed my anger.

"Little Jappy Boy, open your eyes real big. Open them as big as you can. I bet you can't get them to normal size."

The first day in school was the loneliest, most painful, most decisive I have ever experienced. From that day on I came to feel that my parents were right: I had to overcome prejudice by proving myself as good as or better than the others. And prove it I meant to do.

The next morning I rose, full of apprehension, to prepare for school again. I put on a pair of Levis my mother had purchased for me the night before, relieved that I didn't have to wear faded pants that might cause more laughter. Classes went smoothly for me on the second day. The novelty of having a Japanese American in the classroom to tease seemed to have quickly worn off. Students for the most part left me alone. But trouble came when my class in physical education began. As I walked to the gymnasium to report for roll call, a tall skinny boy with a tiny dot of a head, about two years older than me and looking very much like a long-legged spider, approached. Chewing his gum loudly he said, "Hey, kid. Give me your Levis' tag!"

I learned later that anyone who collected five of these tags received a free pair of Levis.

"No, I'd rather keep it, if you don't mind," I replied. I didn't care about the tag itself. It was the way he asked and the way he chewed his gum that made me refuse.

"Aw, c'mon, let me have it."

"No," I said firmly.

"Look, kid, you better give it to me or I'll have to take it from you. Do you want that?" Spider threatened me.

"You can't have it," I said. Spider looked at me and decided I was not going to give him the tag. So he went to get one of his friends. When I saw them coming, I decided I'd better make a run for it. I took off; they raced after me. Round and around we ran. Not able to capture me by themselves, they called for help from a third boy, and the chase continued. Finally they trapped me near the football field. Tired and out of breath, I had no more energy to run and they closed in on me. While two grabbed me and held me down, the third ripped off the tag. I resisted with all my might, but by then my strength had ebbed to almost nothing. Feeling the heavy knees of the boys pressing down into my back, my arms twisted around, I once again was overcome by a sense of chagrin and hatred so deep that I trembled. I lay there in the dust for several minutes after the three boys left. Then I got up, almost in a state of unconsciousness, and tried to brush the dirt off my new Levis.

At that moment I hated whites more than I ever imagined I could. Through these experiences I was rapidly becoming toughened to prejudice and hardened in my

capacity for hatred. That day as I walked home from
school, two boys tried to provoke me with the usual name
calling and insults. Brooding about the events of the past
two days, I grew angrier and angrier at the two white boys
tagging after me. When name calling failed, they started
to pinch and shove me. Then they squeezed me between
them. I threw down my books and put up my fists, ready
to fight. Although I had never once fought with anyone,
I was half out of my mind with fury. "Come on you cow-
ards," I yelled. "Come on and fight."

The two boys stepped back, surprised at the sudden
eruption from a boy who had been silent until then. "There
are two of us here," one warned, "and we're going to whip
you good."

"Just try it," I growled. "You lay your filthy hands on
me again and I'll kill you with my bare hands. I swear I'll
kill you. Both of you. Or you'll have to kill me first."

The two boys looked at me a second. "He's bluffing,"
one of them said. The other, looking more cautiously at me,
said in a slightly scared voice, "Hey, this guy's crazy. He's
not kidding. We'd better leave him alone." With that they
walked off.

The entire first week of school in Pasadena was agony.
It was so traumatic in fact that it was the start of a number
of bad dreams I have had off and on relating to my racial
"freakishness." One of the most bizarre and terrifying
nightmares was that of being pursued in Communist China
by white American soldiers as a suspected undercover agent
for the Chinese government. In an equally fearful dream
I witnessed the explosion of the A-bomb in Hiroshima; in
the middle of the terrifying mushroom cloud amid cries of
death and destruction appeared the weeping face of Jesus

Christ. During that week I also felt an inexpressible sense of futility and fear settle over me as a result of a repetitive dream: As my brother and I were eating ruffled potato chips, I noticed to my horror that latticelike potato chips were slowly coming down like latches between his eyelids and eyeballs. I struggled fiercely to stop them from covering his eyes. "It's no use," he said resignedly, "nothing can change my eyes." I protested, "No, no, you must try," when suddenly I felt the same latticelike latches closing over my own eyes. Desperately I tried to hold them up but found I couldn't. I felt I was forever doomed to look at life with Oriental eyes through American ruffled potato chips. Amusing though aspects of the dream appear, this nightmare left me in a cold, shivering sweat with my heart pounding frightfully.

The dreams underscored the basic ambivalence I felt about myself and my Japanese heritage. Aggravated by innumerable painful experiences such as those my family and I encountered in Pasadena, this ambivalence caused what might be termed a mild case of schizophrenia in which my feelings swung wildly from one extreme to another. There were times when I cursed the Japanese in me for making me a cultural half-breed; but there were other times when I was happy to belong to the Japanese-American community and felt nothing but fury at white Americans for failing to accept me just as I was, a Japanese-American nisei.

Sometimes, out of self-pity and anger, I actually looked for evidences of prejudice to confirm my notions of being unjustly victimized. Fortunately on those occasions close white friends, whose opinions mattered to me, often restored much-needed perspective and prevented me from sinking too deeply in my own small mire of hurts. Nisei friends also pointed out, probably correctly, that the traumas the postwar generation of Japanese Americans face are mild in comparison to what the prewar group had to put up with. But recognition of the relative improvement of attitudes toward Japanese Americans since the war could do little to alleviate my own psychological tensions or to relieve me of a feeling of alienation. This awareness only made me wonder how any people could have submitted to such inhuman treatment. While I do not doubt that anti-Oriental hostilities have decreased markedly since the end of the war, I cannot bring myself to accept emotionally the Japanese-American legend, no matter how much progress has been made in this area. Until true racial tolerance exists, the Japanese-American legend will remain attractive, perhaps reassuring, but exactly what, to a large extent, it is now: American-style fiction at its fanciful best.

8

Ivy League
Nisei

THE INTERNAL CONFLICTS and ambivalences arising from my racial background were not problems that suddenly disappeared after winning acceptance in white circles. Even though acceptance was a big boost to my confidence, the tensions remained unresolved and I tried, unsuccessfully, to cope with them by turning away from the ethnic heritage that stood in the way of complete integration. I made no effort to learn anything about my ancestral motherland, and since there seemed to be little purpose or reward in making the attempt, I continued to demonstrate a deliberately indifferent attitude during most of my youth.

Nor, even had I had the will, would there have been much opportunity to study about Japan through the channels of secondary education, for the overwhelming emphasis in my high school on American and Western European civilization left immense gaps in course offerings concerning Asia, Africa, and Latin America. It now seems incredible that I could have passed through twelve years of education without having so much as one history course designed to introduce the non-Western portion of the globe where over two-thirds of the human race resides. Schooled in this parochial framework, I went to college ignorant about the nation where my parents had grown up.

This state of affairs might have continued had it not been for my first advisor at Princeton University, which I entered in the fall of 1960. By coincidence this young professor, a specialist in Middle Eastern studies, had just returned from a trip to Japan the week before I arrived on campus. So utterly enchanted by the Land of the Rising Sun was he that very little else came up in the course of our consultation. When he realized how little I knew of Japan, he virtually ordered me to enroll in Japanese-language and East Asian-history courses, calling it a crime that I should have lived so long without a sense of my own past. My initial reaction was to resist his strongly phrased advice, but after repeated prodding I finally consented to fit several courses on the Orient into my academic schedule.

My first lecture on ancient Asian history was delivered by Professor Marius Jansen, a kindly, erudite scholar, who lectured about the "great tradition" in East Asian civilization, the impact of contact with the West, and the force of this on the process of modernization. I was thoroughly entranced. The course not only introduced me to the great civilizations that have flourished in East Asia, but radically widened the narrow, Western-oriented frame of reference through which I had looked at the world. From an intellectual as well as personal perspective this was an exciting discovery. For a nisei whose sense of history was shaped by America, it was an astonishing revelation to read about the Edo period in Japan, which by itself was longer than the whole history of the United States Government. The personal curiosity aroused by this course stimulated me intellectually and by the time I was a sophomore I had decided upon history and East Asian studies as my major.

In order to concentrate on Japanese studies, intensive language training was of course a requisite tool. At first I thought Japanese would be easy; many of the words were familiar to me because I had heard Japanese spoken around me as a child. After the introductory three or four lessons, however, Japanese unexpectedly became the toughest course on my curriculum. Because I was a Japanese American everyone assumed that I would have no trouble with the language. But, outside the prewar generation of nisei who studied at language schools or spoke Japanese at home, this assumption was a gross misconception; in fact, postwar nisei generally have a harder time with the language than Caucasians. Because others expect us to speak Japanese fluently, we feel retarded when we cannot measure up to their expectations.

Even those with some background in the spoken language usually find Japanese increasingly frustrating and tend to become discouraged when they discover it is not quite as simple as the language they were used to speaking and hearing at home. Futhermore, many never rid themselves of the bad habit, developed at home, of using a bastardized form of English-Japanese. One of my nisei friends, for example, commented to a visitor from Japan in typical pidgin-Japanese, *"Boku wa* (I) college *de* Japanese *o* study *shite iru* but Japanese *o* house *de ammari* speak *shinai* (don't) *kara totemo muzukashii* (very difficult), I think." A white friend who overheard that chuckled and said, "Gee, I can understand Japanese. It's easy."

Moreover, nisei do not seem to derive much psychological satisfaction, still less emotional exhilaration, from learning Japanese. Many of my Caucasian friends who study the language feel a great sense of achievement when they can read and write the strange-looking Chinese characters. As most Japanese Americans have seen *kanji* (Sino-Japanese characters) since they were children, they do not regard them as particularly exotic. When they study the characters along with *katakana* and *hiragana* (the two phonetic scripts) somehow they think they are learning something they should already know. And, because of their hang-ups on ethnicity, nisei almost never turn into the kind of exuberant Japanophiles, wholly infatuated with all things Japanese, that Caucasians are apt to become.

Among several languages I have studied, Japanese is without a doubt the most complicated. In addition to the difficult characters, various historical forms, and an almost sadistic set of grammatical rules, it involves learning a whole culture, one whose nature is very different from any in the West. My command of Japanese never seemed adequate; everytime I reached a point where I thought I had mastered one aspect, I would face an entirely new and confounding form from another historical period. Unlike French, German, or other "easy" languages that my friends could speak fluently after two or three years, I never seemed to make a breakthrough in Japanese. If only my Japanese genes could actually facilitate the task of perfecting this inscrutable tongue!

By immersing myself in the study of Japan, I was able to rid myself of the many trite stereotypes that unfortunately distort the realities of the country. After clearing away the clichés, I could better understand the Japanese-American subculture as well as the particular values and characteristics that had constituted part of my rearing. I could also handle the conflicts and ambivalent feelings involving my race with greater equanimity as I began to see that there was so much in the Japanese tradition that I could take pride in. Japan's involvement in World War II—about which I was made to feel ashamed during my childhood—was only a brief period in its long history, arising from an arabesque chain of circumstances and events in the context of which it is exceedingly difficult to fix total blame on the deviousness of the Japanese. My old Pearl Harbor-fixated sense of history underwent a profound transformation as aspects of Japan's rich culture were revealed to me, and I realized just how much World War II and ignorance had warped my entire image of Japan. Though not a permanent remedy for problems of identity, this awakening was nevertheless therapeutic in relieving some of the chronic misconceptions closely connected with my unwillingness to accept a dual identity.

At Princeton—reputed to be a school for the upper class —I was one of only five or so Japanese Americans. Although the aristocratic legend is largely erroneous, an anachronistic carry-over from the days of F. Scott Fitzgerald, the Eastern world of the Ivy League was certainly a dazzling one for a West Coast nisei whose only social contact with thoroughbreds had been at the Santa Anita stables. In the midst of this white, intellectual, and in some senses, social elite I felt rather like a rooster in a peacock's nest.

There were countless reminders of how alien I was, by social background and race, in this cream-of-the-crop world. Even the names of college classmates spoke to me of high social birth because of the II's or III's and sometimes

IV's that often followed their names. Not having a post-name title trailing after me like a long royal cape dragging along the floor made me feel somewhat less than presentable in their company. There were times, I must admit, when I could not resist the temptation of imagining how my name would look with a II or III after it. How nice it might be, I occasionally thought, to have lineage and tradition indicated in one's name rather than the incongruous combination of a Western first name and Japanese surname, obviously intended for an immigrant's son. "Daniel I. Okimoto III?" I tossed the idea around in my head and moved my lips silently. But during those flights of fantasy I would come crashing back to reality with the recollection of my birth at the Santa Anita Racetrack and how my name was tied to rather unique circumstances. Daniel I. Okimoto III? Ridiculous. About as appropriate as Donald Duck III.

During my undergraduate years at Princeton and later as a graduate student at Harvard, I was treated on the whole as an individual and integrated within the white-elite society. The atmosphere toward minority races in the Ivy League is exceptionally liberal. Since 1960, with Martin Luther King's dramatization of the plight of minority races, student recruitment from low-income and ghetto areas has become extremely active. In this respect, as in others, the Ivy League took the lead by setting an example for the rest of the nation's universities.

Some prejudice, to be sure, exists even in the amiable milieu of the East Coast. One nisei friend, for example, was actually asked by his roommates to dress up in a white dinner jacket and pose as a houseboy in order to impress some visiting coeds; the nisei laughed good-naturedly as most Japanese Americans are expected to, but the suggestion, even though intended as a practical joke, hurt and angered him much more than he let on. If I had any illusions that racial open-mindedness was a function of education, I soon lost them through such incidents as one in which an acquaintance at Harvard persistently called me "boy," as if using my first name would demean his position in society, or the countless times students with no malicious intent used "Nip" or similar nicknames to show others how funny they could be. And there were many times when I despaired of students who, trying to mimic Asian accents, had no idea how tiring and utterly devoid of humor their antics were.

But these were only minor irritations. My most disagreeable encounter with prejudice took place during my sophomore year at Princeton in a process, appropriately called "bicker," by which second-year students are chosen for membership in eating clubs. Because I always disliked the idea of rah-rah fraternal organizations, I made up my mind early not to participate in the bicker selection processes. Yet, because I was indecisive and easily swayed by group pressures, I compromised individual conscience and succumbed to arguments that I should not try to rock the boat. I went through with bicker, against the dictates of good judgment, and like most of my classmates, became wrapped up in the tidal wave of emotionalism that follows the sending out of bids. Among the bids I received was one from a club renowned as prestigious and Southern. This was apparently the first year a nonwhite had been asked into membership and I suppose I should have felt honored. But the prospect of entering a social group that had refused to admit Orientals and blacks was less than enticing.

When a member came around to ask if I would accept the honor of joining his club, I purposely asked whether they had ever admitted a black. When he said no, I asked why not. Since it was social club, he explained, their purpose was not to integrate the world. All they wanted was a congenial group whose common denominator was a desire to socialize. Hence inviting blacks over the objections of some members would be provoking unnecessary trouble. When I asked if he thought that was right, he shifted the subject by reassuring me not to worry because it had nothing to do with my being Japanese. When my name had come up for a club vote along with that of a Chinese-American classmate, he admitted, several had voiced their objections. But since the rest of the club wanted us, these students had magnanimously swallowed their pride and expressed their willingness to accept us just as we were and to treat us as equals in the club. Though they preferred not to admit blacks, they did not mind having a few "high-class Orientals" to diversify the membership. The Chinese American and I were so offended we vowed that if no black, then certainly no yellow.

The encounter should have been sufficient to confirm my original misgivings about eating clubs, but flattered by the pats on the back by clubs vying for new members, I agreed to enter a club on the rationalization that it would be useless to buck the established social system. Although I felt some initial pangs of uneasiness about acceding to pressures, I later came to feel quite content in the atmosphere of the club. There was a certain sense of security in belonging to an elite white membership as well as no small self-pride in having made it. Consciousness of status so inflated my self-satisfaction that the issue involving the acceptance of yellows but not blacks was all but ignored. I made the adjustment to the eating-club system—but only by abandoning such "incidentals" as principle and concern.

But being one of only a handful of nisei at Princeton was not entirely without its lighter moments. One such instance came when the Assistant Dean of the College asked me to speak before the Board of Trustees.

"I'll be happy to. What's the subject?" I asked.

"Princeton as Asians see it," he replied, puffing on his mellow-smelling pipe, looking every bit a college dean.

"Sir, I'm afraid I don't qualify for the assignment."

"What do you mean?" he replied, puzzled.

"You see, sir, I'm not really an Asian."

"What? Then what are you?" he challenged.

"Just an American," I replied apologetically, "in disguise."

9

Japanese Students in Revolt

IN THE SPRING of 1968 I entered Tokyo University, Japan's proud answer to the Ivy League, as a graduate research student in history and international relations. At Todai (as Tokyo University is usually referred to) there were no racial tensions similar to those that rack numerous American universities, because outside a small body of foreign students the student body is solidly Japanese. Consequently I never experienced distasteful episodes stemming from racial prejudice that would set me apart and make me feel different from others.

This is not to say that the Japanese are free of ethnocentricity. They are not; for on the Todai campus I was sometimes conscious of another type of differentiation: nationality. The fact that I was an American national in a Japanese university was often apparent in my contacts with other students, just as it was in the linguistic fumblings with which communication and research were carried on. While

Japanese students were both cordial and helpful once a friendship was launched, they could also be stiff and sometimes hostile, particularly if they adhered to a dogmatic form of Marxism that encouraged less than kindly attitudes toward Americans. The tendency to form cliques placed further obstacles in the way of breaking into student circles. Unless one belonged to study or extracurricular organizations, it was easy to feel removed and to walk around campus like a stranger on the outer perimeter of the university's activities.

The timing of my arrival on campus coincided almost exactly with the commencement of an intense, year-long student strike that spread rapidly to over 110 universities— or roughly ten percent of all institutions of higher learning in Japan. The strike made it perfectly clear that even though Todai is untroubled by deep racial conflicts, such as erupted at Cornell University in 1969, it is gripped by underlying tensions of its own that may be equally imposing and difficult to solve. The way in which today's Japanese students are responding to these university and social problems is very untypical of the role traditionally assigned the young. They represent a new, postwar generation—impatient with social imperfections, critical of traditional values, and no longer content to conform blindly to the social system. Like some of the postwar breed of nisei in America who are becoming increasingly vocal about social injustices and human rights, these students are militantly involved in many of the pressing issues confronting society. As I found myself squarely in the midst of the tumultuous strike and witnessed the students in action, my old concepts of Japan and the Japanese underwent further modification.

Though the sources of the students' eruption were long in brewing, the strike was precipitated in the medical department when, in June 1968, a group of students seized Yasuda Hall, one of the important administrative buildings on campus, in protest against punishment meted out to several students for agitating against the so-called feudal practices of the department. To clear out the protestors, who stoutly refusing to be budged, the president of the university called riot police onto campus for the first time in its postwar history. The summoning of riot police was widely denounced by radical and moderate alike as a threat to the principle of university autonomy. Instead of ending the sit-in, the move touched off a paroxysm of reaction in virtually all of the school's nine departments. One department after another, seizing on the police issue to highlight more general discontent, voted to go on indefinite strike until an apology for bringing in police was issued by the administration, punishment of the medical students withdrawn, and unpopular practices reformed.

The outbreak of the massive protest left Todai completely paralyzed for nearly a year. During this time campus tensions drew unusual attention from the mass media. Almost every day meetings, rallies, and demonstrations were held on campus. The air was pierced by shrill voices blaring forth agitation over portable loudspeakers. Whenever I went to school, it was not to attend seminars or read in the library, which was barricaded, but to do "research" on student strikes. By observing these events I probably learned more about Japan than a year's digging in documentary resources could have turned up.

Students participated in the strike for a variety of reasons. Some hoped to reform what they considered outdated educational policies; others protested concrete issues such as the introduction of police on campus. The most radical, enamored of a Maoist brand of thought, sought to create a campus base from which to revolutionize the nation's "rotten capitalistic-imperialistic structure." As the strike wore on, campus grievances became increasingly entangled with broader socio-political issues.

In this sense the students were aware that the decade of the seventies may represent a critical crossroads in Japan's postwar history. For two and one-half decades the country has been engaged in the monumental processes of reconstruction; during this time economic, social, and political changes perhaps as far-reaching and permanent as any in its long history have taken place. During the seventies basic decisions will have to be made on a range of issues that will strongly influence the nation's future orientation, and the students of the sixties meant to register their views. These issues include the possible dissolution of the U.S.-Japan Mutual Security Treaty, the extent of military rearmament, the possibility of nuclearization, the degree of economic assistance to and penetration of Southeast Asia, relations with Communist China, and the distribution of Japan's burgeoning national wealth—all important questions with worldwide repercussions.

In the midst of the turmoil Todai's aging president was replaced by a younger, more aggressive successor under whose administration attempts for a resolution were hastened. In mid-January 1969, capitalizing on growing dissension within the ranks of the striking students, the new president held a mass-bargaining session with students at which a compromise settlement of the long list of student grievances was signed. Known as the *kakuninsho* (confirmation document) the central terms included: withdrawal of punishment against the medical students, promises in principle to avoid calling police to settle campus conflicts, pledges not to assist police in investigations of student activities, recommendations to loosen restrictions on student self-governing activities, consideration of student participation in matters pertaining to administration.

Following the signing of the kakuninsho, resolute steps were taken to terminate the student revolt with all possible speed. Most students, mollified by the settlement and eager to resume their studies, voted to end the strike and reopen classes. Alienated now from administration and fellow students alike, hard-core radicals braced themselves to go down fighting, their ranks fortified by activists from other universities and youth organizations. Riot police, which had helped ignite the strike, now came in to subdue the last remnants of opposition. Lifting barricade after barricade, the police laid siege to the final student stronghold, Yasuda Hall. In a fierce battle involving helicopters, water hoses, tear gas, staves, rocks, and Molotov cocktails, riot squads stormed into the building and cleared out the last radical resistance.

Cleaning up the rubble and repairing the destroyed property took armies of workers several weeks. Despite the nominal return of normalcy to the campus, entrance examinations had to be canceled, classes continued for months to be disrupted, graduation ceremonies were suspended, and many other functions were postponed for fear of rekindling the disturbance. During the long struggle, a year of study and faculty research was squandered, hundreds of thousands of dollars were wasted, and physical and emotional anguish was sustained by all involved.

The tragedy of the situation is the present uncertainty whether or not this costly travail has given birth to lasting reforms within the educational and social structure. Some gains appear to have been made, the most significant of which is the sudden increase in concern over problems that disturb the young. But only the most gullible believe the fundamental ailments that led to the ordeal have been remedied. Left untended these ailments could produce imbalances that might prove in the long run even more disruptive and harmful than the strike.

Broadly, the maladies diagnosed by the students fall into two categories: educational and political. In both areas the students have legitimate cause to complain. In the field of university education, perhaps the most conspicuous and pressing problem is inadequate financing. Every institution of higher learning in Japan suffers from a critical shortage of funds to meet the spiraling costs of first-rate research and education. State-supported universities have the soundest financial footing and they are, not surprisingly, the best schools in Japan. Nonetheless, even national institutions do not always get the funds needed to train their students properly.

Private universities face an even graver economic squeeze. Although the enormous expansion of the student population has been absorbed primarily by private colleges through increased enrollment or the opening of new schools, they receive but a meager pittance of support from the government. In 1966, for example, the net amount of federal aid to private education came to only slightly over ten million dollars. Obviously, to insure quality as well as quantity, private schools will have to receive greater government subsidies. A healthy educational system must include vigorous public and private institutions of higher learning.

However, since financial dependency opens an avenue for undesirable governmental interference in the content of education, it might be better if greater financial support flowed from civilian coffers: educational funds, business contributions, alumni and individual gifts. Loyal private support is one reason universities in America like Harvard, which boasts an endowment of over one billion dollars, can stay in the forefront of education. In Japan private contributions to colleges have been severely hampered—indeed, practically prohibited—by archaic tax laws under whose provisions donations are not deductible. Businessmen have told me that contributions to education would be out of the question under present circumstances. There is scant justification for this discrimination in view of the immense tax deductions allowed companies for entertainment expenses. Even though recent ceilings have been set for entertainment exemptions—up to ten percent of a company's budget—Japan's tax structure encourages millions to pour into the vast world of cabarets, night clubs, bars, and geisha houses. These benefit enormously from the windfall of Japan's mighty economic growth—while colleges languish from a critical deficiency of money. An example of this situation is the fact that business in 1969 spent more on entertainment than the total amount government gave over to education.

Faced with the threat of imminent financial collapse, many colleges have resorted to such desperate stopgap measures as expanding enrollment and hiking tuition. But these moves often create more problems than they solve. An expansion of students might stave off impending bankruptcy, but it promotes overcrowding and mass-production techniques of instruction, and leads to no lasting solvency. Nor are economic woes alleviated by raising fees, for families are then forced to shoulder an unjustly high portion of college costs, turning education, in effect, into a luxury of the wealthy rather than a right of all.

Shifting financial burdens onto the very people who often can least afford them could have deleterious repercussions in a democratic nation that depends upon the availability of quality education for all classes of its people. I have wondered at times whether, given my father's small ministerial salary, I could have gone to college in Japan if I had been raised there. In America we were all able to attend universities in spite of our limited budget, thanks to generous financial aid. Unless Japan does something soon to develop an adequate, effective scholarship system, higher education may become increasingly inaccessible for students from low-income families.

Signs of impoverishment are visible in the run-down physical state of most Japanese campuses—even Todai. I sensed a monetary pinch the moment I passed through Todai's red entrance gate. In spite of the university's preeminence in the academic world, its physical facilities fail to convey a stateliness commensurate with its lofty position. Indeed, the campus resembles more a jumble of decrepit, prewar government office buildings than the pride of Japan's education hierarchy.

Construction funds, however, seem to have been poured into new science buildings. The nonscience buildings on campus are notably ugly; most are dilapidated brick edifices wholly devoid of architectural imagination. And if the outside environment is dreary, the rooms and corridors are absolutely depressing. Drab, cramped, and badly equipped, some class and lecture rooms are in worse condition than the tiny classrooms of my grammar school; the state of the facilities at the secondary schools I attended were superior to those I used at Todai. To think that such shabby rooms house what are reputed to be the brightest students in the country is hardly a flattering commentary on the state of higher education in Japan.

Small wonder collegians have revolted against the decaying educational setup; when the third wealthiest country in the world cannot provide decent facilities for its premier institution, something is basically wrong. If Japan were an underdeveloped nation with severely limited funds, the present state of negligence might be understandable. But in view of its actual wealth, one can only conclude that the Japanese government has misplaced its values by placing learning low on the scale of priorities. This is particularly surprising to me since I know from the values passed on to me from my issei parents just how highly the Japanese regard education. There is almost no sacrifice too great among issei to put their sons through college.

But Japan's educational malaise is not just financial; problems extend to the very core of the system, specifically to the institution called "examination hell," according to which admission to all schools from kindergarten to college is determined by rigorous examinations. Once a child reaches grammar school age he begins the descent into this excruciating, many-layered hell. With each advancement in grade level the descent grows steeper and the competition more intense. By the time the student reaches high school, frenzied test preparations turn into a wild stampede for the narrow gates of college entrance.

Coming at a formative period in life, test hell is a tortuous process for young Japanese, particularly the college bound. It demands sacrifices that can adversely effect physical health and emotional development. A number of my friends, even many who succeeded in gaining entrance into Todai, find it painful to talk about the years of arduous study and self-denial that preceded college. They tell me how lucky I am to have been educated in a country where the pressures to get into college are not so intense or unrelenting. Seeing exactly what is at stake for Japanese youth, I too feel fortunate to have escaped the ordeal of sitting for entrance exams. The competition is grueling, and in spite of the yearly toll in emotional stress and suicides, it has continued basically unchanged.

It puzzled me at first that the education-minded Japanese allowed this system to continue operating without at least some modification. Of all people, I would have thought the parents of school-age children—who witness the terrible strain to which their offspring are subjected— would bring powerful pressures to bear against the test-hell route. Sadly, Japanese parents, like their issei counterparts, are more interested in seeing their children succeed within the old system than in initiating reform measures. Passivity is the primary reason for accepting the old order of things; it boils down to the familiar attitude of *shikata ga nai,* or nothing can be done about it. Also involved is the same dogged drive for social success that characterized issei ambitions for their children. Anxious for their own to get ahead in society, Japanese parents, especially mothers, encourage and cajole their children into going all out to pass the exams. The way mothers flock to exam centers and weep or rejoice over the results might lead one to think it was they, not their children, who failed or passed the battery of tests.

The pressure parents place upon their children to pass within the established rules of the game is not only a central reason why exam hell is perpetuated from year to year but also a source of utilitarian attitudes toward education. Most parents look upon college more as a springboard for lucrative employment than as a once-in-a-lifetime opportunity for youth to probe the wonders of the universe. What they want for their children is that all-important graduation diploma, without which social advancement would be extremely difficult. They know there is no faster route up the ladder than admission to the "right school," one, that is, with the most advantageous connections for employment. One mother told me she was willing to pay almost any price to get her son into Todai. Why? Because Todai provides the best connections and the most prestige.

Once the son is in school, it doesn't really matter whether he is educated or not, just as long as he picks up his diploma. For too many graduates the sheepskin might as well read "A.B. in Comic Books," or "M.A. in Mah-jongg"; if it is certified, that is all that counts. They will get good jobs. This holds especially true if they are alumni of Todai, the dream university for all ambitious parents, from whose hallowed halls march 20 percent of all Diet members, nearly all the postwar prime ministers, 30 percent of the presidents of large firms, 30 percent of the top bureaucrats, and 30 percent of all college professors. "Students at Todai," commented one proud father, "really have it made."

The undisputed efficacy of the Todai degree notwithstanding, many students at the university feel less than happy about the quality of education they are receiving. Several acquaintances have pinpointed specific weaknesses in Japan's best-known center of learning. They criticize, for example, administrative stagnancy, saying that during the strike administrators appeared jealous of their prerogatives and slow to respond to voices for reform even though the need was pressing. Complacent about the school's enormous prestige, the administration demonstrated little ability to communicate with students, particularly when compared to the forward-looking policies of universities in the West. For many Japanese students, the employees of the Ministry of Education who handle the administrative responsibilities are no more than crusty bureaucrats whose prime concern is to placate government displeasure by stifling cries for change.

Nor does the faculty command the respect it once did. According to some students who were eager for the strike to be settled as quickly as possible, the faculty's lack of courage and foresight compounded the problem of a communication gap: not enough professors were prepared to interact with students. The faculty should be the cutting edge for the removal of such appendages as the *kozasei* (a system whereby a professor has absolute control over a subordinate team of researchers, assistants, and finances), such debilitating practices as the almost exclusive employment of Todai graduates on the faculty (inbreeding is 95.3 percent at Todai, surely one of the highest figures in the world), and such malignant imbalances as the unfavorable student-teacher ratio (in the law faculty it is about 60:1).

But at the height of the strike the faculty proved singularly unable to act as a catalyst for reform. Instead of responding resolutely, they broke into squabbling factions, feuding as much among themselves as they did with students and administration. Most students to whom I have talked remain skeptical about whether or not the faculty will be able to spearhead the movement to alter traditional student-teacher relations or to promote university or national reforms. Their performance under fire has been discouraging. Several Todai acquaintances lost what respect they had for professors when they saw their weak-willed response to the strike.

Students also complain—with justification—about the curriculum. Over the years the undergraduate course of study has undergone only minor changes despite the tremendous innovations in learning that have been taking place in colleges around the world. Centered around lectures and formal requirements, the curriculum has failed to keep up with refinements in the techniques of education characteristic of other institutions in the world. Students say that not enough emphasis is placed upon small-group sessions. Nor is there any spirit of experimentation—the kind that would lead to abolishing some of the dated, formal requirements and place more stress on independent research. At a time when universities in the West are encouraging student-organized seminars, pass-fail grading, and work-study programs as part of an attempt to infuse greater flexibility into college education, Todai's curriculum remains isolated from evolutionary change.

It is against this educational background that Todai students went on strike. From what I have seen of the situation, I sympathize with their disgruntlement. Their strike in protest against these shortcomings has exposed chronic ailments to public scrutiny, forcing school and government authorities to grapple with the issue of rehabilitation. Authorities have, predictably, balked at most of the significant proposals for reform. And the government, instead of asking *why* students were moved to protest so passionately, hastily concentrated on ways to *put down* university disturbances. Blaming students for rioting, chiding school officials for failing to take stronger punitive measures, the conservative Liberal-Democratic Party (LDP) government enacted stricter legislation, which they euphemistically spoke of as an "aspirin tablet," to bring down the "fever" of striking schools. To the great dismay of students, the government also increased the number of riot police to a point where there is now one policeman for every 600 persons.

This is precisely the kind of response that has embittered the majority of Japanese students toward the LDP government. To comprehend fully the radicalism of certain student groups, in fact, it is necessary to view educational discontent against the larger backdrop of politics in Japan, for long-smoldering resentment against the conservative policies of the government was an important factor in the severity of the strike.

In the West, Japan is loudly proclaimed as the single Asian nation that, despite a vastly different native tradition, has successfully adopted a democratic system of government. But whether this government, as it now operates, deserves to be called "democratic" or not can be debated, depending upon the definition that is applied. There is, for example, no two-party system, traditionally associated with successful democracies in England and America. One powerful party, the LDP, has virtually monopolized Japanese politics since its formation in 1955, and with one brief exception, opposition forces have been consistently incapable of sharing in the leadership. The dangers of authoritarianism growing out of the prolonged dominance of one party are mitigated somewhat by intense factional competition within the LDP broadly involving mainstream and antimainstream forces, but the uninterrupted rule of the LDP clearly involves hazards to the health of a system in which power, ideally, should change hands periodically in response to issues and popular will.

Although statistics in recent elections suggest that the grip of the LDP may be easing somewhat, the polarization of opposition parties will probably impede the establishment of a viable two-party structure of government. So long as power shifts only within a single party from one factional coalition to another, the LDP will have the stength to ignore parliamentary processes when necessary by ramming through legislation in spite of the unified opposition of all the other political parties combined. It is not uncommon to see Diet sessions thrown into utter turbulence by elderly Diet members brawling over the forcible passage of certain legislation. Small wonder young students are skeptical about the supposedly democratic processes of government.

It is an old saying in politics that power corrupts. If corruption is measured in terms of shady political machinations, scandals, hairline differences between legal and illegal practices, and instances of public malfeasance, then the adage can be applied with some accuracy to Japanese politics. Every time I pick up Japanese newspapers, it seems, I read about the uncovering of new cases of bribery, nepotism, and illegal excercise of power. A distressingly large number of politicians within both the LDP and opposition ranks seem to lack individual moral consciences about their public responsibilities. The fear of accepting bribes rises, it seems, less from a troubled conscience than from the possibility of getting caught. Many politicians appear to be just what newspaper pictures show: corpulent old men lacking any guiding concept of public service and more concerned with personal and factional interests than with those of the public. They are shown sitting complacently in deep soft chairs, arms extended royally on rests, their bearing devoid of any spirit of youth, charisma, or vitality, looking indeed as if it would take extraordinary effort for them simply to rise from their comfortable seats.

So rife are political scandals that the Japanese public, which is lenient anyway, seems to have grown immune to their occurrence. "Isn't that what politicians are? Corrupt? —You've got to expect it," commented a friend whose idealism seemed to have been permanently crushed by today's common political practices. Resigning themselves to corruption as an almost unchangeable fact of life, Japanese citizens indirectly abet it by returning to office men of questionable integrity, some of whom have known criminal pasts. It no longer surprises me, as it did when I first traveled to Japan, that some Japanese almost despise politicians. Given the malpractices and the lack of commitment to democratic ideals, it is hard to blame young students for holding politicians in very low esteem or for looking upon Japan's "democratic" politics as a cesspool of corruption.

A democratic government is theoretically one which responds to the will of the people. Here, too, Japanese students have reason to question the degree to which Japan has been democratized. The business of running the country from day to day is left in the capable hands of the

bureaucrats who staff the key ministries of Japan. Ironically, the very efficiency of the elitist bureaucracy may be a
stumbling block, in one sense, to the evolution of a people's
government, for policies are shaped by civil servants in conjunction with business and political elites, sometimes in
diametrical opposition to popular will.

Further distance is placed between power and the people
by the extraordinarily close relationship which exists between big business and government. Fears of excessive
federal control do not seem to trouble business circles.
Cooperation, overlapping interests, and federal paternal-
ism have been features of ties between industry and government since the Meiji period. Although perhaps an economic necessity immediately after the war, this incestuous
relationship has led not only to graft, but to the formation
of an oligarchy of power from which the Japanese people
feel cut off. So close are many bureaucrats to big business
that when they retire from government service they move
immediately into executive positions in the large firms they
have been dealing with for years.

To be sure, the Japanese people themselves must be held
accountable in large measure for the failure of democracy
to sink deep roots. Their reluctance to participate en-
ergetically in the political processes, their general indiffer-
ence to policies, and their passivity in the face of growing
central authority must be counted as major factors in their
alienation from decision making. These and other impedi-
ments must be overcome before democracy is ever fully
realized in Japan.

It is significant that students struck at Todai, for it is this
institution which feeds the national elite with a continuing
supply of fresh talent. In terms of education and employ-

ment, Todai students had the least to complain about and stood to gain the most by not striking. They needed only to conform to the school system while awaiting graduation into the ranks of government and business. But, unhappy with the status quo, they chose to put assured personal futures on the line in order to reform their school and society. Some of my friends risked supremely desirable jobs—such as in the Finance Ministry—others were willing to sacrifice a full year of school, still others fought family and social pressures to abide by their ideals. Their determination to act, regardless of the personal consequences, was an example of courage worthy of admiration. In a country where roles are so clearly defined—and the one assigned to students traditionally covers leisure, passivity, freedom from responsibility, and voicelessness—the striking students at Todai have discarded old images and perhaps opened the way for new modes of action based upon a broad sense of social commitment.

Looking at the student movement from the standpoint of a Japanese American, I am encouraged by the assertion of universalistic concepts like individual rights against authority. I believe this is a healthy development. Like the recent ferment among postwar nisei in Los Angeles, student unrest at Todai has demonstrated that political timidity and passive conservatism are not incorrigible cultural characteristics of the Japanese. The young generation of Japanese, like their racial brothers in America, has expressed its dissatisfaction at playing the traditional role of political eunuch. Authorities in the university and government would do well to ponder causes sufficient to motivate the young to jeopardize career interests in a prolonged and bitter school strike.

On the other hand, lest the mistaken impression be conveyed that the adult world is the sole culprit behind campus troubles, let me hasten to assign students their just share of responsibility. Students have not always made solutions for complex problems easy. In fact the extreme dogmatism and intransigent self-righteousness, together with the counterproductive tactics employed by the most radical of students, have exacerbated disputes and perhaps weakened the liberal cause in the long run. Reacting to the ultrarightism of the prewar period, college students have tended to embrace a Marxist-Leninist view of the world. Many campus radicals today have veered even farther left by subscribing to a variation of M-L (Mao-Leninist) thought. Ideological, generational, and broad international changes have seriously fractured the left-wing movement, creating a gap between the New and Old Left that may never be closed. Radical students deride the old school of leftists who advocate revolution within the existing structure of society. Dedicated to ideological "purity," these students have made pronouncements, full of hackneyed and imprecise terminology, which resound with a virulence and unrealism that badly need the temperance of critical thought.

A major hazard of this type of ideological dogmatism, one to which many of these self-proclaimed revolutionaries have fallen, is the fanatical intolerance it breeds toward contending viewpoints; if there are clashes in opinion, the tendency is to dismiss other views as uninformed or plainly ridiculous. So obsessed by their self-righteousness are some campus activists that no sense of humility, nor allowances for human frailty, nor recognition of the multiple dimensions of truth deter them from their holy crusade. They march out to "enlighten" all those who do not share their views with emotional and, if necessary, physical arguments. While they profess to act for the good of the people, they have managed to alienate themselves from, and earn the disapproval of, the large majority of the population.

The other danger of self-righteousness is the temptation to rely upon violence. The naked use of force in my opinion is not in itself always wrong; much depends on the circumstances. There are situations, I admit, where limited violence can attract sufficient public attention to bring about an ultimate solution; many activists feel that force is the only effective means available to carry on their struggle against an otherwise unresponsive government.

Some overzealous groups, however, have clearly abused the rationale of force, encroaching upon the rights of others, and endangering the noble purposes for which they purport to be struggling. Those students who have made violence a habit may have done the liberal movement a great disservice; in fact, liberalism may have reached a peak years ago that it will not approach for some time to come. What many have failed to recognize in brandishing force is its inherent limitations—indeed, its counterproductivity—as a leverage for reform within an industrialized state. Repeated recourse to violent tactics could undermine, and already has undermined, the effectiveness of the student movement. It has legitimized calls for "law and order," which has led to increasing police suppression, the arrest of several leaders, and effective crushing of the student revolt. Excesses of the left-wing could also create conditions suitable for the resurgence of strong, right-wing nationalism, a force of mounting and as yet unknowable influence in Japanese politics.

This is especially true if nothing more than destruction is the goal of violence. Mouthing Mao's dictum that whole-scale razing must precede construction, revolutionary students appear determined to tear down the social order without having a clear blueprint of what will be erected in its stead. These students obviously lack a sense of history, for numerous examples can be cited to show that what usually follows in the wake of mindless destruction is chaos and anarchy, breeding grounds for totalitarianism.

On the other hand, if violence is to be avoided, the onus of action rests squarely on the shoulders of the so-called Establishment. Authorities in Japan—politicians seated complacently in white-covered chairs, company presidents chauffered around in sleek Rolls-Royces, university administrators hoarding power—had better take heed of the widespread disgruntlement of the young. Whether the enormous energy unleashed in the student strikes can be harnessed toward constructive ends depends in the long run at least as much on the adult world as on the students themselves. Just how adults will react to the student turbulence of 1968-69 will be worthy of close attention for all those concerned about Japan's future course. With the need for remedial treatment of so many vital areas pressing, it remains a question whether the government will recognize quickly enough that "aspirin legislation" may relieve headaches, but cannot cure the malignancy of long-ignored social and educational tensions in Japan.

10

Mother
Society

JAPAN IS KNOWN ABROAD as a male paradise, a land where women are dominated, practically tyrannized. "The Japanese have the right idea," an American once observed. "It's not like America where women completely control their men. Japanese women are not yet tainted with the equality-of-sexes nonsense; they keep quiet, stay in their proper places, and submit obediently, as they should, to the will of men."

From my observations, this stereotyped image of Japanese women is not altogether accurate. Although women in Japan probably do not enjoy the breadth of freedom of their American counterparts, it is misleading to believe they are entirely voiceless or without influence. A more active behind-the-scenes force than is commonly realized, demure Japanese women in their own quiet way exert a strong influence over all aspects of society, especially over the family.

The primary nuclear unit in most societies, the family, is especially important in Japan as a matrix for molding individual character, human relationships, and social consciousness. Tightly knit family units are closely interwoven in the fabric of Japan's social structure, providing cohesion and stability as well as an unusual degree of continuity in the midst of shifting patterns of change.

At the heart of the Japanese household is the mother; to her fall the multiple tasks of managing the household; she is wife, mother, educator, disciplinarian, arbitrator, cook, cleaner, accountant, doctor, counselor, and best friend. While it is the father's responsibility to bring in a steady income, the mother's duty is to see that the money is apportioned wisely in meeting the needs of the family. The husband leaves domestic affairs more completely in the wife's hands than is the case in America where the two have roles which often overlap. Whereas American husbands might assume part of the burden of raising children, shopping, cleaning, washing, and cooking, in Japan the wife would consider such assistance an intrusion since it would represent an embarrassing admission that she has been remiss in her responsibilities as wife and mother. To the Japanese woman, caring for the family is much more than an imprisoning routine for which husbandly help must be solicited. It is her responsibility, her fulfillment as a person—in brief, it is her whole womanhood.

Through her domestic role the wife commands more leverage over her man than quaint pictures of white-powdered, kimono-clad women trotting meekly a few yards behind their husbands suggest. True, the manner in which they get their way may be less obvious than that of many American wives, yet it is not ineffective. While American women might resort to nagging, whining, complaining, yelling, or arguing abrasively with their husbands, forcing a confrontation of wills and sometimes voices, Japanese wives will often use tactics which are less frontal—such as sulking, playing martyr, or repressing anger. They do not demand or expect to share totally their husbands' lives, and their capacity for *gaman* (perseverance) is boundless, but when they really want something Japanese women have a potent arsenal of ways of getting it. If husbands care about peace under their roofs, they will listen carefully to their spouses.

Within the family the woman's prime function is giving birth and rearing children. No other realm of her being—not career, nor interests, nor socializing, nor even wifely duties—consumes such quantities of time and energy. The father naturally also takes a hand in raising his offspring, but as he is often away at work the rearing responsibilities fall largely on the shoulders of his wife. The woman hurls herself into the maternal role with an awesomeness of purpose and feeling.

The resulting mother-child relationship is in my opinion one of the keys to understanding Japanese character as well as the dynamics of social action. For the emotional components of this dependency are carried into adulthood, instilling in Japanese an exceedingly high need for emotional security and affecting the whole nature of human associations. As a consequence society is in a sense deeply feminine; it is a mother society, so to speak, apart from which many Japanese, like children separated from maternal security, feel lonely and disoriented.

From the moment of birth the mother's bond with her child is exceptionally close; the intensity of this relationship is surprising even to someone who has been accustomed to seeing intimate mother-child ties among Japanese-

American families. From infancy to school age, the two are bound together so strongly that one seems almost a physical extension of the other. Foreigners are immediately struck in Japan by the manner in which mothers carry their young strapped to their backs wherever they go. The infant's sense of identity, his orientation to the outside world cannot help but be intimately intertwined with his mother when he is smothered in her unconditional love. It is almost as if the child's period of gestation in the womb were prolonged several years by the extreme closeness.

To Western eyes the degree of tolerance allowed Japanese children appears almost unlimited. Mothers pamper their young, responding like overwrought hens to their every outcry. Babies are forever being talked to, carried, and permitted liberties unthinkable to Western parents—they are thoroughly indulged. Rarely are they wheeled about in carriages, ignored when crying, or penalized for misbehaving. It is the Japanese view that small children should be loved above all, even at the risk of overindulgence. Childhood is not a Spartan training period in preparation for the rigors of adulthood; children cannot be expected to behave maturely when their fundamental instincts and needs are emotional.

However, as children near school age their freedom becomes rapidly saddled with restrictions. Once caught in the hell of school examinations the carefree days of childhood fade to an idyllic memory of the past. Family duties and social responsibilities gradually weigh the adolescent down, bringing the tensions and strains of adulthood.

Compared to America, Japan is a haven for the very young and the aged; both age groups are showered with attention that is denied people in between. Because Japan honors the extreme periods in the human cycle, it is not surprising that these age groups appear far better cared for than their counterparts in the United States. America is a land dominated by teen-age and young-adult culture, and childhood is merely a prelude to adolescence, to be outgrown as quickly as possible, while old age is the much-feared finale of loneliness and senility, to be endured until the end.

Given this difference in stress, the American style of rearing children differs significantly from Japanese methods. In America, the child is not raised so single-handedly by the mother. Nor is he viewed as a lovely but helpless dependent; from an early age he is treated as an individual whose will and mind should be nurtured separately from those of his parents. Trying to bring their offspring rapidly to maturity, American parents generally aim for a balance between love and discipline, guidance and independence, freedom and restriction, tolerance and indulgence on the assumption that the child's life should be, as soon as possible, his own to lead.

In spite of my parents' background, I was raised more in the American than Japanese tradition. As both my parents were ordained ministers whose life mission was to spread Christianity, my mother never centered her life around her children with the single-mindedness of Japanese mothers. Since our home was often located next to the church, my father was always around while I was growing up and consequently was more involved in the tasks of raising us, particularly as a disciplinarian, than most Japanese fathers.

My parents' ministerial calling influenced not only the circumstances but also the nature of our upbringing. They raised us sternly, trying to instill Christian faith, discipline, independence, and self-reasoning, while expecting us to behave like adults even while we were small children. Although in my childhood I did not feel deprived of their love, I never felt stifled by it. Their aim was to mold me into a strong Christian *individual* whose love for God transcended everything else. Consequently my upbringing departed from usual Japanese patterns by being geared not to satisfy parental authority as an act of filial piety, but rather to square away individual conscience with a higher moral authority: God.

In this sense I escaped the suffocating maternal control under which most Japanese children are placed. The Japanese mother wields an immense coercive hold over her child; the love that binds the two together can become a rein with which to lead the youngster in desired directions. Should the child rebel, the Japanese mother, who excels at the art of persuasion, lulls the child with words, coaxing him into behaving. If persuasion fails, she can resort to discipline. If that too fails, she can manipulate his deepest emotions by demonstrating how disobedience wounds her. Maternal tears can stir intolerable uneasiness in the rebellious child and work to bring him around to her will.

Sensitivity to feminine authority is carried in varying forms throughout life. Signs of it are abundant even in adult Japanese society, as for example in the type of advertisements circulated in the mass media, many of which appeal in one way or another to the latent need for feminine assurances. Female voices, whether low, comforting grandmotherly types or the high-pitched, girlish variety, pour out of the radio networks, recommending this department store or that restaurant. Maternal figures are captured in pictures advertising this beef stew or that cough medicine, while little children run around on TV calling nostalgically for *okasan* (mother) to feed them a certain brand of noodles. No less common are the family programs in which matronly figures dominate, appealing apparently to the innermost recesses of the Japanese psyche.

Such advertisements offer striking contrasts to those numerous American commercials that ruthlessly assault personal privacy by seeking to exploit the secret fears of the American people. Given the frequency of their appearance, it is a wonder all Americans are not walking bundles of complexes and hidden fears regarding bad breath, yellow dentures, strong body odors, unkempt hair, dandruff, tired blood, insomnia, and blemished complexions.

The intensity of mother-child ties is vividly seen in the underlying emotionalism and childlike search for security of the Japanese. This aspect of the Japanese character, though deep seated, may not be immediately obvious since the Japanese are masters at hiding their true feelings behind expressionless masks. Masks, significantly, are used in several art forms, such as Noh, and are common literary themes. Stoic expressions may be the reason Westerners complain of Oriental inscrutability; seeing only a frozen face it is difficult for one to know what is passing through a Japanese person's mind. Americans, by contrast, fizzle over with emotion like a shaken bottle of Coca-Cola.

However, behind their masks the Japanese are highly emotional. While nodding and maintaining an impassive front, they may be seething with anger inside. The Japanese have a rather low level of verbal aggression, but when the limits of tolerance have been reached they suddenly explode. To his astonishment a Westerner may find himself confronted with an enraged Japanese, yelling uncontrollably like a child throwing a temper tantrum. Once this point is reached it is impossible to deal with him rationally. He will often pout even after he has regained control of his rage, mumbling to himself and withdrawing from adult means of communication.

Because of their great need for emotional security, Japanese are occasionally unable to cope with conflict situations, as illustrated by their intolerance for diverging viewpoints. Differences of opinion can generate antagonisms sufficient, if not to sever relations, to prevent contacts from becoming too personal. Japanese generally prefer to circumvent head-on clashes, going to great lengths to minimize or disguise disagreements. One of the hardest lessons I had to learn in Japan was to phrase my views as cautiously as possible or rely on circumlocutions when differences had arisen in order to control the danger of discussion flaring into open and heated argument. Accustomed to rigorous but impersonal verbal jousting in America, I have had some unpleasant experiences in which my pointed rhetoric has inflicted wounds that have taken time to heal. However delicately stated, arguments are always potential seeds of misunderstanding on the part of Japanese, who easily interpret honest, impersonal disagreements as attacks on their own dignity and intelligence; the distinction between objective criticism and subjective accusations with hostile intent is a hard one for many to draw.

On top of this, Japanese are often hard to talk with because of emotional predispositions which cloud strictly objective evaluations. It is no accident that the word "open-mindedness" cannot be rendered precisely into everyday language. Although the Japanese excel at academic disciplines that require sophisticated rational thought, like mathematics, they are not always capable of separating reason from emotion in discussion. Intellectual thought, it must be recalled, never passed through an Age of Reason in Japan as in the West, where rationalism was exalted as an ultimate good; even today reason alone is not particularly highly esteemed. Strong undercurrents of irrationalism, and outright antirationalism, flow beneath a good deal of contemporary thinking.

Had I been brought up in Japan, I would undoubtedly look at its society from a wholly different perspective, finding it, as most natives do, more congenial and less atavistic than those of Western nations. I am always somewhat surprised at the pride with which the Japanese speak of their nation as the freest society in the world. For most the mere thought of living permanently in another country is not desirable; the vast majority of Japanese would not trade their society for any other. Although from a constitutional standpoint Japan may indeed be among the freest nations on the globe, it impresses me in terms of *actual* individual latitude as one of the most repressive.

This society, to begin with, is a bewildering labyrinth of human relations, all designed to satisfy the need for security. Each member is bound by a vast network of commitments and obligations, arising out of complicated human affiliations that involve family, work, college, organizations, and friends. Seldom is a Japanese fully free to act as he pleases; he must weigh what consequences his actions will have on an entire range of associates. This tangle of human affairs, which has historic roots reaching back to medieval times, means that many social situations, even today, are laden with vestiges of feudal ties. Asking a simple favor, for example, can invite obligations of sufficient magnitude to discourage a person from making the request at all.

In Japan more than in America connections with the "right people" count as an immense advantage. An introduction from the right man can gain one entrance into college, employment, promotions, favors, privileges, even wives. There have been times, for example, when I have been denied the privilege of using scholarly facilities; try to secure permission as I might, I was always refused. But in true Japanese fashion, I quickly learned, a strategically placed phone call or letter from an influential person could magically open doors.

To function efficiently in such a society the Japanese must think in terms of who and how important a person is. Such calculations seem coldly utilitarian to me and I would resent being strapped by the need to consider friendships beyond simply likes and dislikes. The baroque nature of their human relations denies Japanese the liberty of picking and choosing according to their tastes, forcing them instead to mute criticisms and continue useful associations no matter how unpleasant; discarding a contact simply on account of personal dislike may be a form of social suicide.

Social behavior is further complicated by the penchant of the Japanese for forming cliques. Upon close inspection, nearly all organizations can be seen to be composites of many interacting factions. In the case of political groups, both the Liberal-Democratic Party and the Japan Socialist Party, Japan's two largest, are so riddled with cliquism that no Westerner can properly understand them without first grasping the intricate interaction of their many separate factions. The LDP and JSP are better thought of as federations of factions working together within larger party units than as monolithic entities.

School, political, business, ideological, as well as a myriad of other cliques exist in intense competition within the structure of society. Although cliques may serve some positive functions, their impact on balance is negative, particularly in view of the disunity, corruption, and inefficiency they breed. Given the prevalence of factionalism, it is somewhat surprising that overall social unity is maintained.

However, in spite of the centrifugal pulls of particular factions and groupings within society, Japan is, overall, a very cohesive nation. In this so-called age of discontinuity Japan is in the unusual position of commanding a remarkable degree of unity, which comes from a variety of unique factors. Its population, to begin with, is extraordinarily homogeneous in terms of race and culture; this in itself precludes enormous racial tensions like those that threaten to divide, if not destroy, American society. Furthermore, the dangers of individual alienation are to a large extent offset by the tight network of social organizations which are consciously modeled after maternal, family-type patterns, and these are bound together in a society that offers individuals security within the confines of the group. The citizens are, moreover, very loyal to the nation, and this loyalty, combined with the highest rate of literacy in the world, makes the Japanese willing and able to be readily mobilized to tackle the many problems involved in continuing growth. The easy tendency for certain disaffected individuals and groups to denounce and give up altogether on America in the face of unresolved problems could seriously paralyze American society's ability to deal with tensions in the future; confronted with severe social dislocations, the Japanese are far more likely to pull together than apart.

Tensions, both social and personal, are further affected by such practices as social ritual and role playing. Good form governs a host of social occasions ranging from business contacts to the introduction of friends. The Japanese seem to have just the proper words for the proper situations, the right angle and duration of bowing, the appropriate gift, the fitting routine of formalities. It all has become so ingrained that these practices are almost motor responses. So much social activity in Japan strikes me as ritualization, pure form, an unending charade—void of meaning except when unobserved—but this reaction is probably due to my own limitations deriving from my upbringing in a society that relies far less heavily upon forms. In a crowded country like Japan, where people have to live and work together interdependently, some ritualization is essential for the maintenance of social harmony. Forms not only protect what privacy can be salvaged, but help to relieve tensions that arise from close contact and threaten to disrupt human relations. Hence, though social ceremonies may seem vacuous and troublesome to an impatient nisei, they function as lubricants for social interaction in Japan.

For over 250 years Japan was organized along the lines of a rigid hierarchy, buttressed by Confucian ideology, with clear vertical distinctions drawn between classes. A century after the end of the Edo period, Japan is still to a large extent structured vertically in a "modernized" hierarchy. The top political party is the LDP, the top steel company Shin Nippon, the top bank Fuji, the top advertising company Dentsu, the top university Todai.

Within organizations there is also a clear ranking system that places people into vertical pigeon holes. Yet this ranking system does not mean that people in superior positions lord it over those below them, because superiors are expected to be as concerned for their inferiors as the converse relationship. In fact, the danger of any one person or group, however highly placed, wielding dictatorial authority in most organizations is limited because such high value is placed upon the wishes and well-being of those under them. In many organizations leaders are frequently honorary figures whose prime functions are to represent the group and to oversee its harmonious operation. Power, like responsibility, is hard to pinpoint because it is so widely diffused. In many of Japan's important bureaucracies, ideas and proposals generally are initiated at the lower levels of authority and work their way up rather than percolating downward as in the West.

Nevertheless, the adjustment to hierarchical orderings has not been particularly easy for a nisei like myself. Because Americans are not used to thinking of vertically ranked relations in the same way as Japanese, I have had trouble adjusting to the *modus operandi* of Japanese society. English is not a language which forces the user to conceptualize in hierarchical terms, but the very nature of Japanese imposes social distinctions. In the simple act of choosing words one is faced with the problem of selecting levels of politeness appropriate for the position of the person to whom he is talking.* It is this aspect of the language that I have found the most mystifying. I feel fundamentally uncomfortable having to make social evaluations through

*The Japanese language is, however, changing in response to rapid changes taking place in social relationships.

the medium of speech. Because the American style of social intercourse has instilled notions of equality, it feels as unnatural to speak down to someone as to speak up to him. At first I tried to skirt this problem by using polite forms with everyone, but I discovered that this tended to keep relations stiff, forcing others to match the level at which I was speaking. Then I tried to use informal forms consistently, but that only irritated older, "socially superior" people.

Consequently I now reluctantly apply general distinctions between close friends (with whom I speak informal Japanese) and acquaintances, strangers, older people (with whom I use a more formal idiom). Being a nisei, I am forgiven for lapses and inconsistencies. Japanese assume I just do not know any better; sometimes I do not, but usually I *prefer* impropriety to hard-line social classification.

For a native who must live and work in this vertical society, however, carelessness in language can be costly. A section chief *(kacho)* will usually say *O-hayo* (morning) to employees under his supervision. Should a young employee fail to respond consistently with *O-hayo gozaimasu* (good morning) it could cost him the goodwill of his boss, even perhaps a deserved promotion. Being restricted to the use of one acceptable answer might be annoying to Westerners, but the Japanese accept this without much complaint. Indeed, they seem to desire clear social ordering over confused, ambiguous situations in which no definite guidelines for speech or manners exist. In this sense the customary practice of exchanging *meishi* (name cards) provides a convenient means not only to remember names and addresses, but to get an idea of a person's status. On one small card is printed all the raw data needed for an instant assessment of age, educational background, occupation, position, and income. Although an American might be offended by the idea of summing up the value of a person's life on little cards, most Japanese regard it as a useful custom by which to classify status and retain vital information.

Westerners may also be dismayed by certain ceremonial routines so central for social intercourse in Japan. For example, Japanese are inveterate gift-givers, offering presents for every conceivable occasion; failure to present a gift under certain circumstances can constitute a serious breach of manners. Until recently salaried employees received two bonuses a year, part or all of which they were expected to use to purchase presents for their bosses—not just any present, but something that reflected the esteem in which their superiors were held. Though outsiders may find the custom of constant gift-giving bothersome, to the Japanese it is a matter of proper manners and good form.

Being used to such formalities, Japanese would probably find American society slightly uncouth, if not downright crude. To people who are scrupulously careful to avoid officious questions about private matters—like those concerning personal feelings or money—the American fondness for talking boldly about almost any subject would come as quite a cultural shock. In contrast to Japanse *enryobukai* (very reserved) attitudes, Americans feel little reluctance in making inquiries about a person's finances, voicing criticisms, or perhaps prying into personal affairs.

To perpetuate social harmony and order, role playing is heavily relied upon in conjunction with ritualized forms. Social roles, based on such criteria as occupation, status, and age, are neatly defined and faithfully enacted. For each position, it seems, a distinct image has been created; from this set image behavior usually deviates only within a tolerable range of acceptability. The Japanese can adapt themselves to fit rigid molds partly because they are other-directed personalities—that is, people whose actions are guided more by the opinion of others than by internal dictates. At the root of the Japanese character is an anemic sense of individuality that is constantly defined in terms of conformity to particularistic social norms. Perhaps it is no exaggeration to say that in Japan stronger emphasis is given the role than the individual.

The stress on social propriety over personal conscience hinders the emergence of strong individualists; in fact, the sense of identity of the Japanese is confused when cut off from the security of clear-cut social contexts. It is significant that while there is an abundance of richly descriptive words for socially sanctioned behavior, the Japanese terms for "self," "self-identity," and "individualism" are vague and not commonly heard. The words that smack of individuality—such as *kojinshugi* and *kosei*—generally convey nuances of selfishness and egotism.

The problem of an individual identity, independent of social approbation, is a theme which emerges repeatedly in modern Japanese literature. A common pattern in novels is for the protagonist to get lost in deepening caverns of self-absorption, searching for an exit from the haunting questions: Who am I? Why am I living? In many cases the way out of this consuming existential quest is never found. The hero in works by some of Japan's leading novelists is left tormented by a confused concept of himself and his relationship to society. Unable to establish a satisfactory individual identity apart from society, from which he feels alienated, he loses his sense of direction in winding tunnels of pessimism, leading to darkening nihilism, disillusionment with himself and others, and ultimately to the final negation of self through the act of suicide.

Part of the difficulty of forming a hard-core individuality can be traced back to the mother-child relationship. So dependent is the child on his mother from the start that his sense of self, even as he grows into adolescence, continues to depend critically on others in the maternalistic society of which he is a part. Given free rein during his early years, when for all practical purposes the world revolved around his wishes and whims, the Japanese develops an assertive ego that has been carefully nurtured by maternal love. As the child grows older he is trained to satisfy his need for security not just through his mother but through his whole family. Gradually he learns that in order to be sustained in security he must channel and control his ego. He is expected to assume some of the responsibilities of the household and, should there be a conflict of interests, he is rigorously taught to subordinate his will for the higher good of the family. The welfare of the household is given strict precedence over those of its individual members. This is a major difference in the upbringing of nisei and their Japanese counterparts; although taught to honor their families, Japanese Americans generally are not raised to sacrifice their individuality for the benefit of the group.

Subordination of the individual to the family unit is later transferred to other collectivities in society. Personal impulses that interfere with collective interests are suppressed as the group—whether family, social clique, or company—claims priority over the individual. This does not mean, of course, that individual interests do not exist;

in fact, because of the self-centered indulgence permitted them during childhood, Japanese, especially men, are as egotistical and self-seeking in their private ambitions as any Westerner, as indicated by the oft-heard reprimands against *wagamama* (selfishness, willfullness) and *jibunkatte* (egoism, self-centeredness). The Japanese are no less selfish than others, but they have been trained to sublimate and direct their will within collective concerns.

Personal identification with groups is consequently much stronger in Japan than in the United States. Ties to school and company frequently involve deep loyalty and commitment. Their search for security within the group and their sensitivity to the opinions of others make the Japanese touchy about criticisms directed against any group to which they belong, be it family or nation. They want to hear laudable comments about themselves and their country and they take critical, even if honest, evaluations quite personally. Witness the public furor over the unflattering statements about the Japanese made in 1969 by Ichiro Kawasaki (in his book *Japan Unmasked*), who was dismissed as Ambassador to Argentina for his remarks, or the extreme offense taken by many when, in the same year, the British R.S.P.C.A. accused the Japanese of cruelty to animals.

With this overwhelming group orientation, it is understandable that Japanese history does not unfold as a stirring epic of individual heroes who single-handedly alter the course of events; conspicuous by their absence are men like Alexander the Great or Charlemagne. Nor is modern Japanese politics shaped by charismatic individuals such as Mao Tse-tung or Charles DeGaulle. The history of Japan is less a study of individuals than of groups, cliques, families—in short, collective action. And contemporary

Japan is moved not so much by one or two bold individuals as by the sum industry of the entire nation. Decisions are almost always made by general consensus within organizations. Though not particularly distinctive or daring as individuals, the Japanese are nonetheless energetic, bold, and inventive in groups.

While this collective orientation is a powerful stimulus toward social dynamism, it is at the same time a potential source of danger. As evidenced by the remarkable degree of centralized control in Japan even today, the Japanese are highly vulnerable to the authority of the highest collectivity: the state. The idea of inalienable individual rights which must be protected against government encroachment—so essential a concept for democracy—is yet to be firmly implanted in Japanese attitudes. An underdeveloped sense of individual rights, it will be recalled, was a significant factor in the acceptance of internment by the issei and nisei in America.

Perhaps this weak concept of human rights can be attributed in part to the subordinate concept of self, the priority given the group over the individual. To the Japanese an aggressive assertion of individual rights runs counter to his notion of individual subordination and seems wrongfully self-centered. Consequently the very concept of democracy as a dynamic process involving a maze of aggressive, competing self-interests, ultimately checking and balancing each other, is one of the most elusive for the Japanese mind to grasp. So accustomed are they to suppressing threats of self-interest that the idea of openly supporting "selfish" individual impulses smacks of social anarchy.

When Professor Shinkichi Eto, one of Japan's leading

scholars in the field of international relations, introduced the term "national consensus" into the Japanese vocabulary, it was immediately misinterpreted to mean a unanimity of view through the elimination of diverse opinions. This distortion of the word's original meaning is indicative of the Japanese proclivity to value solidarity and harmony over diversity and conflicting views. Members of the LDP government as well as opposition parties have called for national consensus on a broad spectrum of issues; but the phrase as they use it means no more than popular acceptance of their particular programs, obviating the need for dissension-sowing debate. The terms "national consensus" and *kokumin no go-i* (popular consensus)—two pithy slogans in Japan's political parlance—have generally been interpreted as "similarity in views," or even stretched to mean "elimination of individual dissent," instead of a broad concurrence based on the right of dissent and diversity of views.

"I just don't understand how America maintains any solidarity," one Japanese friend remarked. "Americans are so egoistic that I don't see what keeps society from coming apart. Nor do I see how businesses command internal cooperation when their employees have personal rather than company interests at heart. The secret to Japan's economic success has been the channeling of its people's enormous energy and industry through collective action. It couldn't have pulled off its postwar growth without sublimating the individual to the group."

Social sanctions against recalcitrant individuals can be devastating. People who refuse to play roles or to conform to stereotyped images—placing instead their own interests above those of the group—encounter criticism so vitriolic that it can lead to alienation, if not ostracism. Those who dare to be different must possess exceptional confidence and the courage to accept the consequences. Nonconformity based on the dictates of private conscience is exceedingly difficult to maintain in Japan, as documented in the massive failure of individual resistance to prewar military totalitarianism.

Many of the expressions of social rebellion today are either temporary or basically a "conforming nonconformism" rather than genuine manifestations of individualistic sentiment. The *futenzoku* (hippie) movement in Japan, for example, is not so much a spontaneous protest against the nightmare of human mechanization as it is a fashionable scene, a poor attempt to imitate the original movement in America. Futenzoku are not, as in America, middle-class, college-educated flower people rebelling against materialism and phoniness; many are only show-offs and misfits who delude themselves into thinking they are beautiful people because they look odd and defy common norms of hard work, cleanliness, and modesty.

Open attempts to break out of the womb of mother society are seldom successful. Personal release from group pressures is often found only by immersion in accepted but nongroup activities. Nature is one source of solace. As evidenced in the magnificent native art forms, a heightened sensitivity to natural beauty is seen to be a characteristic of Japanese culture. If childishness is perhaps one cost of the national character, an elegant simplicity of taste is the beauty of it. Among the many qualities most endearing about the people is their ability to relish the simple joys of life—a stroll through a garden, a fleeting look at a crane in flight, a sudden glimpse of withered branches silhouetted against a crescent moon. There are probably few people whose emotions are more deeply stirred by the subtle moods of the natural environment than the Japanese.

In the history of Japanese thought the gods, man, and nature have been tied very closely together in a harmonious unity; unlike the West where God and man are separate and man's task is to master nature, in Japan man is an essential part of a unified nature. Meditation in religions like Zen Buddhism is directed toward flashes of perception, abrupt insights into the fundamental oneness of man and his environment. While this view enriched the literary and visual arts, it may have delayed the development of science prior to contact with the West, because one of the fundamental assumptions of science is that nature is both impersonal and consistent, regulated by rational laws which, if discovered, allow man to rule the universe.

In classical Japanese poetry, an art form brought to a high level of refinement, nature as subject, image, and allusion is extraordinarily important; the poet's sense of identification with his environment is much closer than that felt by even the most romantic Western bards. Throughout the embroidered tapestry of Japanese fiction hauntingly lyrical descriptions of nature are found and often, as in the works of Yasunari Kawabata, natural settings create the basic mood for characters and plot.

Art in many forms provides another release for the individual. Through the act of creativity the Japanese can to a certain extent avert the entangling web of social pressures and human relations. Music and sculpture, creations of a single mind, offer routes for individualistic expression. Ceramics, painting, dancing, scholarship, and other pursuits enable individuals to roam about in more spacious lands than the overcrowded society of Japan permits.

Although other, less refined means of escape exist, notably drinking, these are at best temporary. For those to whom nature, art, and creative paths are closed, drunkenness offers a means of unloading woes without incurring the wrath of tolerant peers. When drunk a person can rid himself of personal frustrations and return to his social position the next day with impunity.

If the Japanese had a livelier sense of humor they might be able to survive social pressures with greater individuality left intact. Although they are a happy people with a hearty disposition for laughter, they do not demonstrate any special gift for wit in their daily lives and at times can be serious to the point of lugubriousness. This is a curious phenomenon, for many of the components of humor seem to be present in Japan: a language rich in semantic double and triple meanings (seen in the poetic convention of *makura kotoba*, pillow words or clever puns), social relations ideal for spoofing because of their stress on rituals and stereotyped roles, a basically affirmative, optimistic people. However, except for such professional entertainment as *rakugo* (storytelling which uses subtle wordplay humorously) the Japanese do not display as crisp a sense of wordplay as, say, the English. Rakugo is a specialist's art, confined to the theater, and little punning is heard in everyday conversation.

Comedies, it is true, flood the television and cinema media, but to Western eyes they rely too heavily on slapstick to be very funny: characters pushing each other, shouting insults, and going through tasteless vaudeville routines. Laughs become especially loud when decorum is outrageously broken or when people make fools of themselves. Some of the subtlest and funniest moments in Western films are missed, while Japanese audiences go into convulsions over scenes that Westerners do not consider particularly amusing.

There are several reasons why, by Western standards, the Japanese do not have a keener sense of humor. They lack a philosophical sense of life's ultimate absurdity and without some degree of disengagement from the treadmill of events in life there is often little basis for humor. Nor does the other-directed personality afford the Japanese sufficient latitude to laugh at others or themselves. Being so sensitive to the opinions of peers, the Japanese tend to regard laughter directed at themselves as one of the cruelest possible insults; it slashes at their whole being. In Japanese society, where delicacy is the password in human relations, people are very careful not to crack jokes about others, even when no harm is intended. Light sarcasm and playful banter in all but close relationships merely asks for trouble.

Yet despite the oppressiveness of society, the arabesque complexity of human interaction, and the difficulties of asserting real individualism, when all is said and done Japan's society is from many standpoints one of the world's most dynamic and efficient. The spectacular successes of postwar reconstruction alone stand as stunning proof. Faced with staggering problems—including immense physical destruction, paltry natural resources, and a spiritual vacuum—Japan has rebounded with a resiliency that is one of the impressive stories of contemporary history. It has been able to accommodate far-reaching changes within the stable continuity of tradition more successfully than any other society I am aware of. Indeed Japan at this stage could be better prepared to cope with the bewildering array of problems and dislocations brought about by rapid avances in modern technology than even the United States. Eyes that have been riveted on the models of the West may turn eventually toward Japan for inspiration. It is very possible that Japan will become the pace-setter for nations grappling with problems of social fragmentation and seeking to find answers to the challenge of combining dynamic change with long-term stability.

If my parents had never immigrated I would probably be an insignificant cog in this country, snugly settled in my little social niche. The majority of Japanese seem quite content with their lives. Doubtless many would find America too casual, disjointed, uncultured—in a word, too individualistic—for them to leave the warm womb of Japan to settle in such a chaotic society. Given the security and happiness derived from this maternal society, I can certainly understand this sentiment. I might have shared it if I had been born and raised in the Land of the Rising Sun.

However, as an outsider I could never comfortably fit in, even if the Japanese accepted me as one of them. For having been brought up in America, where informality and individuality are emphasized, I find Japan far too restrictive, group oriented, and coercive. It is secure, to be sure, but for my tastes the security it offers comes at too high a levy on individualism. For native Japanese it may be a mother society, warm and reassuring. But it is not my mother.

11

Japanese-
American
Family

FOR ISSEI WHO LEFT the security of Japan, the adjustment to America was usually not easy. To survive in a society which was in so many ways fundamentally dissimilar to the one they had known, the immigrants were forced to abandon or modify some of the old-country patterns of behavior and orientation. Still, successful adaptation could take place without a wholesale abandoment of their traditional culture in part because some of the values—like achievement orientation—and characteristics like strong family ties were very compatible with those of the society into which they were adopted. The transition from a tightly interwoven, group-centered society to one more loosely knit and individualistic may have been substantially easier than the reverse would have been, and this probably made acculturation without complete sacrifice of old ways easier. Even though there was commonly an abrupt cultural disjunction between issei and nisei, which widened with each generation, many Japanese families in America retained certain characteristics that were originally carried over from Japan.

As American as my own upbringing was, I was nevertheless struck by similarities and parallels between typical family life in Japan and the kind of milieu in which I was reared, particularly in the small northern California city of San Lorenzo, where a fair number of Japanese-American families resided. The majority of these were employed by several local flower nurseries, the town's principle "industry," through which they earned comfortable, if somewhat modest, incomes. The Japanese population was drawn together into a small community within a community, somewhat like Japan's rural villages in having a solidarity all its own.

Certain features of the Japanese community, like living arrangements, set it apart from the larger white population and showed that some old-country practices continued to be adhered to even in the United States. Unless serious internal problems—such as an irresolvable conflict between mother and daughter-in-law—prevented issei from living together with their nisei children and sansei grandchildren, it was quite common for three generations to reside in the same house. Imbued with a strong sense of *oya-koko* (filial piety), the prewar nisei (in contrast to the trend among the postwar generation) did not feel that it was right for their parents to be alone in their old age. Most were willing therefore to put up with daily inconveniences as well as long-lasting tensions in order to accommodate their issei parents.

The issei themselves never failed to impress me with their unflagging capacity for work. It was almost as if they turned around old maxims by living to work rather than the reverse. Instead of resting inactively at home, most were happier to be at their daily jobs well beyond the accepted age of retirement. That way they felt they were doing something constructive, not simply wasting time or waiting around passively for the end to come. The money earned was usually used frugally; despite their advanced age, few felt the compulsion to go on senile splurges. Like the Japanese, the issei displayed a remarkable penchant for saving a high percentage of their salaries—not perhaps for specific purposes so much as simply for the security of having some reserve in the bank. Savings eliminated the need to depend solely on their children, and it meant there would be something to pass on to their heirs.

My family's poverty as well as my father's position as *sensei* (a term of respect usually used for teachers but in this case referring to a minister) made us the object of uncommon concern to the Japanese community in San Lorenzo, just as it had in San Diego. Exceptional effort was exerted to see that we were well cared for. Not only did we receive clothes, books, food, and other essentials but also what amounted to free dental and medical care from nisei doctors whose children attended our church.

The Japanese fondness for gift-giving, the importance of saving face, the highly stylized manner of communication, and other cultural characteristics were features of the ethnic community that were associated with relations among the issei. When, for example, gifts were given to help us through hard times, the issei donors were always careful to protect our pride. Seldom did they fail to explain that they were going to throw away this shirt or book (even though some were obviously new) or that this steak or fish would spoil (even though they might be frozen), so would we be so kind as to relieve them of these things? My parents would initially refuse with apparent finality, but our friends would insist, reiterating that they hated to see things go to waste. If my parents remained stubborn, they would change their tactics and express how deeply indebted they were to us, thus making acceptance a duty rather than an act of selfish volition. By accepting the gift the debt incurred by our friends could be properly returned, and we could feel that it was not a handout that we greedily snapped up. The whole reciprocal-obligation syndrome was in operation among the issei, and as in Japan it was all designed to keep relationships solidified and ultimately to satisfy certain dependency and security needs. It all seemed needlessly rococo to me, but that was the way communication took place.

In San Lorenzo, my father, an avid nature lover, had ample opportunity to develop his gardening interests. After building a sturdy hothouse, he began accumulating a wide assortment of flowers and plants, especially cactus, which he had grown to love during camp days in Poston. Every afternoon at five he interrupted his Bible study to walk out to the garden where he lost himself in the greenery. The plants were like children to him, and he lavished loving attention on them—watering, plotting temperatures on graphs, reading books on botany, grafting, and seeing the products of his labor grow. His particular favorite was *bonsai,* the traditional Japanese miniature trees and plants created in a single small pot. I used to sit and watch him roaming through his hothouse, so intent yet so relaxed, enjoping the simple aleasures of nature. My more pragmatic mother felt he wasted far too much time with his plants; the daily hour spent with them, she believed, could be better used preparing sermons or doing other ministerial tasks. But for my father to spend one hour a day alone with the mysterious creative force of nature, so symphonically seen in the delicate purple trumpet of one orchid, was to know the boundless eternal richness of the universe. In this sense it was almost a religious experience.

Japanese customs were not infrequently, however, a source of embarrassment for me when they were followed outside the ethnic community. My parents' practice, for example, of bringing gifts with them for conferences with my grade school teachers placed me in an awkward position among my classmates. Though the gifts were only token, a gesture of appreciation, the mere act of presenting them, I always feared, might strike my white friends as currying favor. I also felt a child's sense of embarrassment at the unsightly clothes my parents wore and the funny foreign accents with which they spoke to my teacher and friends. My mother in particular looked silly to me, clothed in a drab cotton dress, smiling Orientally out from under the folded visor of a crumpled black hat that had gone out of style back in the thirties, bowing profusely to my teacher and thanking him for putting up with her dim-witted child.

Even when there were instructors whom my parents knew I disliked, they bowed their heads humbly as if the teachers were great Greek philosophers, expressing the hope that I was not causing too much trouble in class with my bad behavior. I knew it was a Japanese custom to say only polite things in front of others, especially before people considered social superiors, but I still resented the exaggerated praise that was always heaped upon people whom I considered undeserving. My parents defended their flattery by pointing out that the occupation was worthy of respect, even if I felt the teacher sometimes was not. They explained that in Japan children are strictly taught to honor their teachers. Not very mindful of the Confucian parent-child hierarchy, I was not beyond blurting out impudently that America wasn't the old country.

"Still, we are Japanese and that's how we ought to act."

"You're Japanese, not me," I sometimes snapped back in angry denial of my Japanese heritage. "I'm an American."

Because of my parents' almost obsessive concern about our educational progress, the days when report cards came out were filled with anxiety. Although good marks were rewarded with kind words and sometimes material gains, bad reports were cause for fear. My father, a stern disciplinarian, sometimes spanked us when we failed to do consistently excellent work at school. My mother punished us in more subtle but even more severe ways by showing us her hurt; instead of physically reprimanding us she simply broke down and cried and made us feel miserably guilty for causing her such grief.

To increase our incentive my parents would resort also to the tactic of comparing us with one another and with other nisei children our ages. If we failed to live up to the standards set before us, we were made to feel as if we had disgraced the family name. Likewise, if some nisei child received better grades, we were always reminded that a little extra effort could spell the difference between greatness and mediocrity. In the presence of issei friends, my parents would eulogize other children while belittling their own. "How I wish my children were as bright as yours. I'm afraid these pumpkin heads just don't measure up." If such comments had been reserved only for us we might have become discouraged rather than stimulated, but since most issei seemed to practice these tactics, and since we knew that our parents were secretly proud of us, the praise and belittlements all evened out and in the end the sense of competition among Japanese-American youngsters became even stronger.

The personal desire to excel was further strengthened in us because we were ministers' children. We were constantly told never to forget that as the issei pastor's children all eyes in the community would be riveted on us. Our behavior and accomplishments had to exemplify the ideals of Christianity or our parents' effectiveness as ministers would be severely handicapped.

Most of the Japanese in the community, if they were churchgoing, attended the Holiness Church. In the absence of other institutional gathering places, the church was in many ways the focus of Japanese-American activity in the small town. Issei parents, even if they weren't Christian themselves, allowed, even encouraged, their children to attend services, thinking it would help them grow up as Americans yet also keep them in touch with fellow Japanese. A great many issei had no strong religious beliefs of their own when they arrived; many were either indifferent religiously or nominally Buddhist. After a period of residence many gravitated to churches which represented the dominant religion of their adopted nation: in Latin America it was Catholicism, in America it was Protestant Christianity. The general tendency was to adapt to the religion of the new nation.

Of course there were some issei who preferred to send their children into San Francisco to attend Buddhist services because they felt it was important to retain Japanese ways. At those churches regular classes were held to provide instruction in the Japanese language. Buddhist services tended, however, to become Americanized, adopting the Christian practices of sermons and hymns in the ceremonies. Some of the hymns even used the same melodies as Christian ones with alterations in the lyrics, such as "Buddha loves me, this I know." In addition to religious worship, ethnic churches, both Buddhist and Christian, helped solidify the subculture and speed acculturation within the broader American society.

One problem that issei, like other immigrant groups, faced was the difficulty of bridging certain gaps with their children. The so-called generation gap, in the case of issei-nisei families in the U.S., should perhaps have been called a "generation jump," for the temporal and cultural differences were far greater than relationships in average American families. There was really a leap of two generations rather than one, approaching more the distance between Caucasian grandparents and grandchildren than between parent and child. The gap was widened often by the tendency of issei men to marry late, resulting in age disparities between father and son not uncommonly of fifty years or more. By the time some of my nisei friends reached twenty, their fathers were already in their seventies.

Language was another formidable barrier between issei and nisei. Not many issei arrived in America with the ability to speak English, and even after thirty or forty years some still cannot carry on simple conversations in English. Whereas prewar nisei can often make themselves understood in Japanese inasmuch as many attended language schools or spoke Japanese at home, few of the postwar nisei can utter more than one or two words of Japanese, still less convey fluently their innermost thoughts. Hence communications present imposing problems between parent and child. Verbal communication often remains on a rather superficial level. The parent is forced to use Japanese to the children and the children English to the parent when discussion turns to weighty matters, the result of this being that neither side can catch the full meaning and nuances of the other. Consequently nonverbal means of conveying feelings—intonations, looks, moods—are heavily relied upon. No matter how effective the nonverbal language, however, the differences of speaking in English and Japanese all too often leave issei and nisei in two separate worlds, each catching only incomplete glimpses of the other, each more apt to leave some of the strongest emotions of his heart—such as love, gratitude, and concern—unsaid rather than to express them clumsily in an inadequate tongue.

In our own family the mode of communication was characteristically Japanese in emphasizing the implicit over the explicit where some of our deepest emotions were involved. Unlike Caucasian families I have visited, which say how much they love each other, hugging and kissing uninhibitedly, we did not lavish words of fondness and respect on each other even though we felt them inside. We just did not feel the need to say the words, because we sensed them intuitively. It would have been as embarrassing for someone in our family to hear words of affection as for another to utter them. This marked aversion for direct declarations of love may seem paradoxical in view of the exaggerated flattery that was freely heaped upon others, but it is actually part of the Japanese pattern of communication and social orientation. The need for reassurances through such values as giri and gimu, rituals, and elaborate means of relating was virtually obviated in the household, for there was an abundance of security within the family.

12

Little
Tokyo

WHEN OUR FAMILY MOVED in 1954 to Pasadena, we found
ourselves in the county that contained the largest concentration of Japanese Americans in the continental United
States. Adjacent areas included, the total number of Japanese Americans in Los Angeles County now exceeds 100,
000, most of whom reside in certain areas like Crenshaw,
Gardena, and Long Beach. Around such densely populated
districts has evolved a subculture that differs from San
Lorenzo's Japanese community in being predominantly
urban, middle class, and vastly larger in scale.

The "capital" of this thriving subculture is an area
affectionately known as Little Tokyo, a small strip of
several blocks in the heart of downtown Los Angeles, just
behind the city's police department and next to Chinatown.
For accuracy the "little" of Little Tokyo should be stressed,
for the four or five blocks of stores and restaurants bear
scant resemblance to the area's mammoth namesake 6,000
miles across the Pacific. East First Street, busiest of Little
Tokyo's blocks, is a drab little street, narrowly passing

between faceless one-story shops whose open doors reveal unimaginative displays of goods marked "Made in Japan." No distinctive character marks the tiny district; one of the few sights that sets it apart is the relative abundance of Japanese ambling silently along the concrete sidewalks.

At small import-export shops Sony transistors are available at prices well above those in Japan and magazines like *Josei Jishin* lie on book counters, picked up now and then by bored customers who flip through the pages, looking for pictures of pretty pinup girls. Close-up portraits of Japanese actresses like Sayuri Yoshinaga can occasionally be seen smiling shyly through display windows, giving Little Tokyo its only loveliness and charm. In cramped restaurants rude waitresses in cheap kimonos, some of whom are divorced war brides, serve second-rate sukiyaki and greasy tempura as the resonant voice of Hibari Misora mingles with the cigarette smoke slowly rising into the air.

Every year toward the end of August a festival called Nisei Week is held in honor of the Japanese Americans in southern California. The seven-day celebration consists of exhibitions, games, talent shows, and a beauty contest in which a local girl is chosen to reign over the occasion as Miss Nisei Week. On the last night a noisy parade caps the week's activities and enlivens the otherwise deadpan atmosphere. Bands, floats, and dancing nisei stream colorfully through the streets, jammed with cheering spectators, and for a few confectionary hours Little Tokyo lights up with something like the gaiety and bustle of its namesake in Japan.

The subculture symbolized by Little Tokyo is one which, considering the great size of Los Angeles County, is remarkably tight and self-contained. Members of this sub-society not only show definite preferences to live near and to socialize with one another, but to conduct commercial transactions with each other as well. Many businesses are geared for Japanese customers, just as a number of nisei professions cater primarily to nisei clientele. It seems that Japanese Americans would rather give their patronage to firms and professionals of their own race either because they consider nisei to be more reliable and honest or simply because they are of the same race. My own parents, for example, did much of their shopping at a store called Tokyo Foods, kept their money in the Sumitomo Bank, went to a nisei optometrist, and called upon the services of Japanese doctors, dentists, and lawyers.

This penchant for sticking together is evident even from a young age. In high schools near Japanese residential areas the large population of nisei students tend to gravitate into nisei cliques that offer both companionship and security. While not all belong to such cliques, those that do are bound together by a strong sense of group allegiance. For outsiders—that is, non-Japanese—it is difficult to break into these closed circles.

Inbreeding is also evident at the college level. The vast majority of nisei college students in southern California prefer to enroll in institutions on the West Coast rather than in other areas of the country. Many who are well qualified to attend Ivy League schools never seriously consider the possibility for fear of not fitting into a predominantly white student body. Parents also fear that the paucity of Japanese Americans in the East merely invites social isolation or intermarriage.

Several California universities, where nisei are particularly abundant, have all-Japanese fraternities and sororities that sponsor parties and dances where members of the opposite sexes can mingle. These social clubs are convenient for those who prefer to date only within their race. Even those who do not narrow their social scope so exclusively often quietly prefer to do the serious work of prospecting for marital partners among their own kind. There are of course a substantial number of Japanese Americans, particularly among the postwar set, whose social companions know no racial boundaries; there is even a small minority that goes to the opposite extreme of refusing to date anyone Oriental. But most of my nisei acquaintances, given the choice, will stick to the subculture for socializing.

Near college campuses it is not uncommon to see entire houses or apartment complexes taken over by Japanese groups that sleep, study, and cook their rice together every day. Nor is it unusual in the large libraries of such universities as Berkeley and U.C.L.A. to see nisei flocking to one side of reading halls or claiming squatters' rights in certain study rooms which other students jokingly recognize as Japanese-occupied territory. This self-imposed segregation is even seen in public areas like the beaches of southern California. Playa Del Rey, near Los Angeles International Airport, is a popular seaside hang out, often crowded with nisei boys playing volleyball or football and pink-polka-dot-bikinied nisei girls lying lazily on beach towels, listening to rock 'n' roll music on their Sony transistors.

I never became part of any nisei in-group. From the day we moved to Pasadena, in fact, I felt myself moving further away from the Japanese-American community, both physically and psychologically, than was ever the case in San Diego or San Lorenzo. This is perhaps ironic since Pasadena placed me in the vicinity of more Japanese than at any time since Poston. Although as many as five or six thousand Japanese lived in the city, the majority of them were settled in the western part of town which meant they not only attended a different high school but also moved among an altogether separate circle of friends. At Pasadena High there was just a handful of nisei, among whom I could count only one or two good friends. Consequently, except for my mother's church, which I attended regularly, my contact with Japanese Americans was very limited indeed.

There were times, of course, like my first year in Pasadena, when I longed for the steadfast friendship of nisei. There is a certain security connected with moving among one's own people, if for no other reason than for the assurance that one will not be maligned or blackballed simply because of race. A shared background often binds nisei together and eliminates any need for them to be withdrawn or on guard against hurt. During the first year of transition, while I was still reeling from the derision of my white classmates, the idea of keeping company with my kind seemed especially enticing. If there had been a clique of Japanese at my school, I undoubtedly would have eagerly sought to nurse my wounds among them.

But since none existed, I was forced to become a loner until I could find a niche in white circles. Once that happened, friendships with whites alleviated the need to go out of my way to find companions among my own race. Indeed, so fulfilling were these associations that I must confess to some feelings of self-congratulation at having made it in the white world; I even passed through a stage in which I not only was not part of the Little Tokyo syndrome but deliberately shunned it. What I felt toward the subculture was aloofness and, if I am honest, a certain amount of scorn for what appeared to be unnecessary clannishness.

Behind these pronounced sentiments, I suppose, lay an assortment of personal hang-ups that had less to do with the subculture itself than with the obstinate problem of identity with which I was struggling. By turning away from contact with groups of Japanese Americans I was seeking perhaps to negate that Asian part of me which stirred such feelings of ambivalence and self-hate. Perhaps I was operating under the illusion that, in contrast to those who accepted their Oriental heritage more openly, I was somehow really a "pure" American, wholly assimilated in the bewitching world of the majority, and that this had been accomplished without having to rely on the security of the nisei community. This attitude was clearly self-deluding, a temporary answer to the schizophrenic tensions which I felt. It was only after I overcame the need to apologize for my ancestry that I lost this false feeling of superiority and came to see the Japanese-American society with some degree of objective perspective.

Looked upon without bias, there can be no denying that, within the sheltered subculture or not, Japanese Americans as a group distinguish themselves through their various achievements at school as well as in their professions. Every year the list of nisei who win prizes in music recitals or garner academic distinctions is long, particularly in proportion to their numbers. It is by no means rare for several nisei to be among the top ten students in some southern California high schools and colleges. In my own graduating class of 1,000 at Pasadena High, there were three Japanese Americans in the top ten even though there were less than ten in the entire class. One of my teachers was so impressed by the performance of his nisei pupils that he once asked me in all seriousness, "Is there any such thing as a stupid Japanese American? I have never in my life run across such a specimen."

The perseverance of the Japanese minority against most discouraging odds in the early half of the twentieth century began to reap big dividends after the war; the postwar generation which knows only part of the hardship and quiet exasperation of its prewar predecessors is the beneficiary of this long-term investment of effort. Partly perhaps as catharsis for a guilty conscience, the Caucasian community has poured out commendations in recognition of the Japanese rags-to-riches story. It is natural perhaps, given the plaudits, for Japanese Americans to feel some sense of pride in their record of accomplishments, Their satisfaction is not the product of blind ethnocentrism; it is based on hard facts, borne out repeatedly by scholarly investigation, and suggested by the proclamation of several sociologists that the history of America's Japanese is a dramatic tale of triumph over adversity, an "unparalleled" success story in U.S. history.

13

The Intolerance
of Success

DESPITE THE OUTPOURING of praise from the white community, my own reactions to the celebrated success story of the Japanese minority are not quite so effusive or one-sided. While the many achievements of this minority should be acknowledged, it must also be pointed out that much of the praise that is showered upon us springs from a fountain-head of middle-class assumptions, some of questionable value, and that these neglect to mention the reverse side of success: the sacrifices that had to be made, the shortcomings that are all but overlooked in our pilgrimage into the Land of Milk and Honey. Since to dwell exclusively on our accomplishments is to present an incomplete picture, some of the less attractive aspects of the Japanese-American pattern of acculturation need to be discussed. Of greatest importance, perhaps, are the costs at which our social advancement has been won.

In adapting to American society, we have had to face the persistent and perplexing problem of how to look upon our dual heritage. The difficulty of reconciling these twin

144

aspects of our lives is often revealed in that moment of hesitation many experience when asked, "What are you?" In my own life there have been times when I have been frankly at a loss how to reply. Depending on my mood and the circumstances, my answers have vacillated between "American," "Japanese," and "Japanese American." Whatever the response, it usually felt somehow unnatural. I never considered myself 100-percent American because of obvious physical differences. Nor did I think of myself as Japanese. The social opprobrium associated with being a member of a minority also made me slightly uncomfortable about declaring myself a Japanese American.

Perhaps this question would not pose such problems if an atmosphere of greater tolerance existed in America. Certainly if the United States were a harmonious melting pot in which all races are accepted equally—as myths would have one believe—there would not be any need to feel hesitant about identifying with a minority, particularly one as successful as the Japanese. But in the face of prejudice it is often hard indeed to resolve the Japanese and American elements.

Like a number of others, I passed through a period when I almost always responded to questions about my nationality with "American." The mere fact of being questioned made me bristle with indignation at the ignorance of those who felt the need to inquire. At the bottom of my eagerness to be recognized as an American, was a deep-seated discomfort about my Asian past. Even at those times when I referred to myself in jest as a "Buddha-head" there was probably some degree of self-derogation.

Unfortunately, as a consequence of this state of mind, we nisei all too frequently attempt to jettison the Asian aspects of our personalities. In our eagerness to scramble to the top of American society, many of us have paid the costly price of abandoning the "baggage" of our cultural heritage, the finest features of which have contributed to the competitive position we now hold. Although Japanese Americans still stick together in closed groups, the substance of our subculture has lost much of its "Japaneseness." Certain old-country stresses, such as that placed on education, survive today, but gradually these have come to be associated less with Japanese-American values than with middle-class American norms.

As any casual conversation will reveal, Japanese Americans are on the whole no better informed about their ancestral homeland than non-Japanese. Few are willing to make an effort to learn anything about it. Although this disinterest may perhaps be inevitable as the struggle to establish an American identity goes on, it is nevertheless a loss to lament, particularly in view of the richness of Japanese culture. Japanese concepts of aesthetics as expressed in such art forms as ink painting, woodblock prints, folkcrafts, traditional gardens, and architecture stand up well in comparison with the world's great artistic achievements. The same can be said of Japanese literature, cinema, martial arts, flower arrangement, tea ceremony, Noh, Kabuki and Bunraku drama, and Zen Buddhism. How unfortunate that so few Japanese Americans consciously seek to keep alive this cultural heritage.

Interestingly, there is a movement taking shape now among the postwar generation to reevaluate the problem of identity and the significance of their ethnicity. No longer apologetic about being members of a minority nor eager to discard their past, many college-age nisei today are rebelling against remnants of racism and old Oriental stereotypes, and are aggressively raising a cry for Yellow Power. Like Afro-American groups, Asian-American organizations are appearing on campuses throughout the country, their members demanding courses that can help them recover a sense of their historical roots. They are redefining their role and place in society and, from a newly delineated perspective, participating in the momentous issues confronting the nation.

The new ethnic consciousness and defiance against racial prejudice owes much to the Black Power movement which, by boldly challenging the status quo, brought vividly to light conditions of injustice that confront all minorities, leading the way for other races to join in the long-delayed fight against discrimination. Borrowing the insights and even some of the rhetoric of the blacks, the Asian-American movement represents a sharp divergence from the old pattern of silence and passivity. While Yellow Power may never become the rallying cry for Orientals in the same way that Black Power has for Negroes, the affirmation of racial ancestry is the kind of major shift in attitude that could have far-reaching implications for Asian subcultures in the United States.

Even though the term "nisei" applies to Japanese in both North and South America, the two groups are quite different in their identification with their Japanese past. Nisei in Latin America appear on the whole to have come under less compulsion to shed their Asian identity than those in North America. Not only do they tend to speak better Japanese, retain more Oriental customs, and maintain closer ties with relatives in Japan, but they also hold their ancestral culture in higher esteem than their counterparts in the States. This may be the result of timing; large-scale immigration to South America took place more recently than that to the United States. But it is probably more directly related to differences in the areas into which Japanese culture was carried. Location helps explain why Japanese Americans on the mainland and in Hawaii are not the same. In the presence of more Japanese and perhaps less anti-Japanese prejudice, Hawaiian nisei seem to retain more of their racial identity, maintain a larger and more cohesive ethnic community, and in general appear less frantic about Americanizing than those on the continent.*

The successes of the Japanese in mainland America have been predicated on a thoroughgoing accommodation to white middle-class norms. The high degree of conformity is evident in the general behavioral patterns of nisei students: in the classroom they are extremely well-behaved, seldom make noise, never talk back to teachers, faithfully finish their school assignments on time. Neatly dressed, cleanly scrubbed, polite and deferential, nisei on the whole would be among the last to join hippie communes or participate in avant garde movements. Although some postwar youths are beginning to defy traditional modes, the majority of Japanese are still the epitome of the clean-cut all-American prototype in all but physical appearance.

Quiet conformity has no doubt helped to minimize social

*Some of the differences between Hawaiian and mainland Japanese are significant enough to merit mention that this discussion of Japanese Americans is based upon the pattern on the mainland, specifically in California. Many of the generalized comments, however, do hold true for both mainland and Hawaiian groups.

deviation and outbreaks of crime; in this sense it has functioned positively in gaining Japanese Americans admission into American society. However, from quite another perspective, the unquestioning, almost mindless acceptance of middle-class standards has given rise to an insensate conservatism that has all but deadened impulses toward individualism and creativity. It is rare to find among the Japanese community individualists who not only think heretically but dare to court strong social disapproval by disregarding convention. Accolades from the Caucasian community, inadvertently perhaps, have reinforced this timidity by convincing Japanese Americans that it is better to be safe than conspicuous. As a result, nisei are proud of their upstanding reputation and are reluctant to risk damaging it with unorthodox activity. Told what exemplary citizens we are, we have responded gratefully by continuing to embrace the order and norms of the white mainstream. How dull the United States would be, I have thought at times, if it were populated only by those of Japanese ancestry.

Given this social orientation it is hardly surprising that artistic creativity, except perhaps in certain fields of the visual arts, is not an attribute for which Japanese Americans are noted. Strict conformity to established norms will probably insure continued prominence in traditional middle-class occupations. Successful nisei dentists, pharmacists, engineers, and businessmen there will always be in great abundance. But the odds are stacked against writers of originality or poets of genius. So long as nisei swallow set standards of social propriety so unquestioningly, so long as they are intent on following the well-worn paths to middle-class success, they will probably lack the raw material of experience, the social relevance, individual perception, and artistic vision, to say nothing of the personal daring needed to assume the high risk of failure, that are basic ingredients for genuine creative expression. Though of course the possibility cannot be ruled out, it appears unlikely that literary figures of comparable stature to those of minorities like the Jews and blacks will emerge to articulate the nisei soul. Japanese Americans will be forced to borrow the voices of James Michener, Jerome Charyn, and other sympathetic novelists to distill their own experience. Even if a nisei of Bernard Malamud's or James Baldwin's talents did appear, he would no doubt have little to say that John O'Hara has not already said.

The drive to adapt to white standards of success has recently prompted some postwar nisei to make the charge that behind our conformity and ambition lies a strong desire to become white. Once securely ensconced in high social positions, some Japanese Americans have become yellow Uncle Toms, or in the lively jargon of the militant young, "bananas"—yellow on the outside, white inside. Currently ranking as Top Banana is S. I. Hayakawa, who was appointed president of San Francisco State College during its bitter strike. Although Dr. Hayakawa became the darling of the silent white majority in California by ripping out wires from student microphones and by following a get-tough policy against recalcitrant blacks, he hardly endeared himself to many postwar nisei who felt he had sold out completely to the white Establishment. To them it was unforgivable that he had callously misused his ethnicity to thwart the aspirations of another minority. They pronounced him guilty of willingly becoming the flunky of reactionary white politicians in need of a Japanese lackey to lead the "holy alliance" against the "lawless" insurrection of the blacks.

Nor is Hayakawa the only banana. Combined with their apolitical bent, the conformity of the Japanese Americans has prevented many from involving themselves in the great social issues facing the nation today. The nisei in southern California seem at times as allergic to liberal causes, such as fair housing and civil rights, as other residents in the area whose reactionary political views are notorious throughout the country. The aversion to participate in just causes is puzzling in light of the historical suffering of the community; but it is yet another aspect of our adaptation that has been largely overlooked.

There are happily some signs of change, at least insofar as self-interests are at stake. The dismissal of Dr. Thomas Noguchi as Los Angeles County Coroner is a case in point. When complaints against the alleged sadism and morbid personality of Dr. Noguchi were made public, many of the good citizens of L.A. screamed for the "Jap's" removal from office. Whether such a hue would have been raised against a white or whether such charges would have been so readily believed is doubtful. Operating on the assumption that a minority suspect is guilty unless proven innocent, the County Board of Supervisors acceded to pressures by dismissing the doctor without investigating carefully the facts of the matter or granting him the right of a public hearing. Although some influential Japanese typically recommended that he accept the dismissal without a fight, thousands of others grouped together in an ad hoc orpanization called JUST—Japanese United in Search of Truth —which collected over 10,000 signatures of protest, raised large sums of money, took the case to court, proved Noguchi's innocence, and won his reinstatement as County Coroner.

However, the nisei community is in little danger of winning medals for social crusading on the behalf of those outside its own circle. Socio-political apathy continues to be one of our most debilitating defects. Lack of concern for fellow humans is graphically captured in the statement I have heard expressed much too often: "We've made it. We've overcome the barriers of racial prejudice without help from anyone else. Why can't the others?" S. I. Hayakawa embodied this hardhearted outlook in its extreme when he simplistically suggested that Negroes emulate nisei in their struggle to find a place in society.

Such attitudes raise the question of whether an ethnic minority such as ours can really be considered successful. True, Japanese Americans have succeeded in securing a comfortable bourgeois life, an accomplishment for which we have earned the rousing commendation of the white majority. But this praise, it must be realized, has been based on value judgments that ultimately serve the purposes of the established social order. Professor Harry Kitano, in his informative book, correctly points out that "the judgment of Japanese Americans as the 'model American minority' is made from a strictly majority point of view. Japanese Americans are good because they conform—they don't make waves—they work hard and are quiet and docile."* When this lauded minority sits back indifferently and says, "We made it, why can't they?" I doubt whether we have succeeded in any but the narrowest materialistic definition of the word. For in a broader

---

*Harry Kitano, *Japanese Americans: The Evolution of a Subculture* (Englewood Cliffs, N.J.: Prentice-Hall, Inc., 1969), p. 146.

spiritual and humanistic sense we have failed abysmally, not only as a minority group but as compassionate human beings.

The spiritual dimension of the nisei success story is obviously as important as the material, yet this aspect is often overlooked by those whose eyes catch only the glitter of our position and possessions. Failure of the human spirit does not register in sociological studies—intangibles of the heart are not amenable to points on a graph or lines on a chart. Ours is not a failure of wrong action; rather it is one of omission, which is no less reprehensible because it involves doing nothing at all. Indeed, passivity in the face of injustice is particularly insidious because it often goes unnoticed or is subject to deceptive rationalization.

Perhaps my reaction to the conservatism and political lethargy of the ethnic community may strike some delicate Japanese Americans, particularly those incorrigible optimists who insist America is indeed the Promised Land, as excessively harsh. But "don't rock the boat," "let them work for it" attitudes strike me as basically immoral. Perhaps this is because my family, having lived in the ghetto after the war, takes the civil rights movement very personally and has become involved in it in one way or another. My brother, Joe, has in effect dedicated his life to working with the poor and oppressed.

After graduating from Harvard Medical School, Joe was moving safely along the established tracks toward the security of a job as a surgeon, a most prestigious and lucrative profession. During his residency, however, he began to feel deeply uneasy about the disconnection between the wonders of modern medicine and the world of human misery inhabited by blacks and other minority groups. Health care seemed to be largely a middle-class luxury, out of the reach of those poverty-stricken people who most needed it. Unhappy with the elitist orientation of the career he was headed for, Joe quit surgery to devote himself to that area of medicine—public health and social medicine—where he believed he could best help the minority races and the poor.

Joe's decision to throw away assured wealth and status was perplexing for many of his colleagues and friends, who could only conclude that he was hopelessly confused. Within their hierarchy of values, he indeed will never reach the pinnacle of success epitomized by a surgical career; nor will he boost statistics about the nisei success story. For Joe, who lived in the slums of San Diego, it is back to the "ghettos, Indian reservations, and other areas of poverty," as he put it in his letter of resignation. This move may be both foolish and foreign to some nisei, particularly those whose prime ambition is to set up practice on East First Street of Little Tokyo, an area about as remote in spirit from the ghettos, Indian reservations, and other areas of poverty as the Japanese Americans are from the struggles of those minorities. But regardless of what others think of him or his decision, he will have the satisfaction of knowing he acted as his heart and conscience dictated.

It is unfortunate that so many nisei, climbing up the social ladder, have given primacy to material over humanistic values. Gradually, many have assumed some of the less desirable features of their newly acquired status. Preoccupied with materialism as are the majority of Americans, many are deeply committed to the stylish life. Comfortable houses, sleek cars, and fashionable clothes are the accouterments of the middle-class success they have pursued so single-mindedly. Conversations with some nisei friends have left me wondering at times whether any values supersede material accumulation in their view.

With the passage of time the Japanese in America have also begun to display more of the patterns of delinquency and crime found in other American groups. Acculturation has resulted in the erosion of some of the principle qualities that set Japanese apart as a particularly law-abiding minority. While crime statistics still fall substantially below other groups', violence and other forms of destructive behavior have become increasingly prevalent. Unthinkable in the past, crime rates and juvenile delinquency have risen to such a point that it is no longer rare to witness gangs of Japanese youngsters marauding through the streets of Los Angeles, fighting with knives and guns, and aimlessly destroying property.

In taking an overview of the Japanese-American road to success it might seem that the pattern of adaptation through passive conformity to the structure and norms of society points beyond the simple abandonment of ethnic legacy and the assumption of certain middle-class values ultimately toward total assimilation. Although there may be a long-term trend in this direction, powerful currents are moving counter to the drift toward assimilation, as shown by the resistance of the subculture to diffusion within the larger framework of society. It is true that the postwar generation of Japanese Americans, unlike the prewar breed, no longer need to band together defensively in the face of such blatant discrimination as existed before the war, yet social barriers continue to exist, and today's generation seems to prefer the company of its kind. Quite apart from the question of whether this is desirable or not, the presently visible evidence indicates that it is premature to forecast dissolution of the Japanese subculture.

The matter of marriage, the key to final assimilation, is a complicated question for which no clear tendencies are discernible. There appears to be a growing open-mindedness about marrying into other racial groups, which is nevertheless offset to a certain extent by definite preferences, even among many of the postwar set, to find spouses within the ethnic community. The whole marriage issue has been, and still is, overladen with all sorts of volatile emotions and stubborn prejudices. Even when young Japanese Americans choose marital partners from the subculture, as many prefer to do, difficult problems can still arise. The issei did not come to America wholly unfettered by social biases; even today issei grandparents occasionally object to marriages involving partners whose ancestry can be traced back to "undesirable" social origins: those from Okinawa or worse, *eta* (outcast class in Japan), are anathema to many issei, who might try to prohibit marriages despite the freedom of the youngsters from such biases.

The situation becomes even more complex when *hakujin* (whites) or *kokujin* (blacks), enter the picture. This is partly because some Japanese Americans continue to harbor a distrustful attitude toward non-Japanese. This defensive suspicion is unlikely to disappear so long as the remnants of anti-Japanese hostility are not erased. The arsenal of arguments against interracial marriage from the standpoint of Japanese Americans is frequently well stocked with racial and social myths, some of which are quite farfetched, concerning the physical incompatibility of races, the alleged ease with which whites divorce, unresolvable differences of background, and social difficulties for mixed children. It is my impression that many nisei parents will try just as hard as, if not more so than, non-Japanese families, to dissuade their children from marrying out of their race. My parents as ministers have frequently been called upon by desperate parents to discourage nisei-white, nisei-Mexican, nisei-Chinese, and sometimes nisei-Negro couples from intermarrying. The tranquility of a number of households has been shattered by the eruption of emotions over prospective non-Japanese in-laws. If persuasion fails, some parents as a last resort will threaten to disown the children. But the passage of time, particularly if a grandchild has been born, generally restores harmony within the family.

The issues of intermarriage and ultimate assimilation, like a host of other complex questions, await answers from future generations of Japanese Americans, beginning with the postwar group now reaching adulthood. The nisei community has come to a new, and in some ways decisive, turning point in its comparatively short history in the United States. The questions that face my generation will undoubtedly require new answers and call for fresh modes of action in determining our future role in American society from those that have brought us to our present position.

The imminent danger that confronts us now is not so much the obstacle of social oppression or the threat of another bitter internment experience or the looming specter of potential failure. Unlike our prewar predecessors we face comfort not hardship, security not uncertainty, and general tolerance not discrimination. Our challenge stems, paradoxically, from an excess of success. The question that will concern us is not whether we can make it in American society, but whether the price of achieving social success is too high. Concretely, this means: Can we receive praise without losing perspective? Can we adjust to middle-class living without necessarily accepting wholesale the inbuilt prejudices and undesirable characteristics? Can we relish our newly won social status and material affluence without forgetting the misfortunes of those who are still seeking them? Can we enjoy our freedom without forgetting the oppression other minorities suffer?

These challenges demand no less determination or courage, because they arise from the very successes that have been passed on to us, than did the imposing barriers that pushed the issei and older-generation nisei to the limits of their abilities. Indeed they are perhaps in the long run even more demanding and difficult, because they represent internal challenges, not external obstructions, involving the human spirit and heart. Whether we possess that extra measure of inner strength and spiritual greatness to rise up to these subtle but stern tests is a matter only the future will tell. Our present response to them, however, will determine whether the much publicized Japanese-American experience is really a success story.

14

A Question of Loyalty

AMONG THE POSTWAR GENERATION in both the United States and Japan, the war in Vietnam, more than any other issue in recent years, has kindled heated debate and consuming passions. In America the war has had a pulverizing effect on old values and accepted legends, and the overall impact has been to shake badly the very confidence of many people in the integrity and moral foundations of the U.S. government. In Japan the repercussions have not been quite as shattering, but there is no doubt that, as a result of U.S. involvement in the war, the image of the United States has been seriously tarnished—which could influence the nature of future relations between the two nations.

The intensity of feelings among the Japanese people concerning the war came as something of a surprise to me when I arrived in 1968, for Prime Minister Sato's declaration of support for America's intervention had given me, and many others, the mistaken impression that the people of Japan were firmly behind U.S. policy. Although the prime minister's statement may have reflected the official

159

sentiments of certain business and government circles, it certainly did not represent the popular opinion of the masses, who were highly critical of U.S. involvement. The mass media missed few occasions to lash out against U.S. aggression; television channels were jammed with special programs featuring gruesome films of Vietnamese who were killed during U.S. bombing raids which, given the heavy casualties in Hiroshima and Nagasaki during World War II, touched off waves of sympathy for the National Liberation Front; countless roundtable discussions were held to consider the full implications of the war, including the dangers involved for Japan in allowing the U.S. military to use Okinawa as a base for bombing missions. The whole atmosphere was charged with emotionalism and the message that got across to me was one of shocked indignation. A journalist summed up the general sentiments of a substantial number of people when he said that before the Vietnam war the Japanese people's judgment of the United States had been much too naïve and trusting.

Feelings ran even stronger, I discovered, at Tokyo University. In the history department, which is known for pronounced left-wing views, I was surrounded by fellow students who denounced the United States in no uncertain terms, calling American intervention "imperialistic" and U.S. refusal to withdraw "immoral." A number of students were members of, or sympathized with, an antiwar organization called Beheiren that demonstrated and worked actively in protest of the war. My own discussions with students turned, almost inevitably, to the topic of Vietnam and frequently unexpected outbursts of anger and resentment were expressed.

The eruption of emotions was not limited only to left-wing Marxists; there were occasions when right-wing students, for very different reasons, suddenly became excited when discussion turned to Vietnam. One quiet, reserved boy whose face was usually as stiff and expressionless as a mask became flushed with obvious anger in talking about the situation in Southeast Asia. Though he was probably not typical of Japanese feelings, he raged against the "arrogance" of a global power like the United States thinking it had the right to "push around" a tiny country like South Vietnam. There was an edge in his voice when he described how he detested seeing American soldiers in Tokyo on leave from Vietnam in search of Japanese girls to satisfy their "animalistic" desires. The sight of them, beer-bellied and hairy, brought back memories of relatives who had been killed in the Second World War. Tears sometimes collected in his eyes, he said, when he was reminded of what foreign soldiers had done not only to Vietnam, but to Okinawa and Japan.

There were not a few whose views of the Vietnam conflict were colored, to some extent, by an element of racial consciousness. Some even came right out with interpretations of the war as an attempt by the whites to keep the yellows suppressed. Although much of the youthful outrage never became known in the United States, a number of students with whom I came into contact confided that, under the impact of the Vietnam war, their impressions of the U.S. changed from goodwill to outright suspicion and scorn. American motives and ambitions in Asia became suspect for these young people. One eminent professor at Tokyo University was troubled by the long-range harm the war had inflicted on America's image; as an illustration, he remarked that the use of the atomic bomb, which had been regarded as a tragic but inescapable consequence of war, was being reinterpreted by a growing number as a barbarous act of genocide against yellow people. This brought home to me the appalling costs at which the war was being waged and merely confirmed the strong objections to the war I felt before going to Japan.

From my own standpoint as an American of Asian ancestry, the basic motivation of our involvement in the war never impressed me as racially inspired, even though old Oriental stereotypes about the Yellow Peril may well have tinged the premises upon which intervention was based. I did, however, object to the government's missionary attitude toward underdeveloped Asian nations and the traces of white-superiority myths. It angered me to hear of some nisei, mistaken as Viet Cong, being shot by fellow American soldiers. It was equally galling to listen to daily news broadcasts of the war which were ended by totaling up casualties in tones that implied that Vietnamese lives were somehow less valuable than American lives; there was an implicit feeling that the staggering toll of South Vietnamese was nothing compared to the list of American dead—almost as if they meant better an Asian dead than an American. Wartime or not, I also found it appalling that Viet Cong deaths were cause for rejoicing rather than mourning. The contempt felt by some American soldiers toward the Vietnamese was enough to rouse suspicions of racism, especially when ugly episodes involving the use of Vietnamese civilians for target practice were revealed.

This war—and all it involved—had a tremendous impact on me, as it did on a whole generation of young Americans, reshaping the way we look at global events, casting doubt on much of what we had been taught to hold sacred, and calling into question our loyalty to the U.S. government. From the start of the large-scale escalation in 1964, our intervention in the civil conflict struck me as a serious mistake. On the basis of my own study of Asia, it seemed that our policy was guided by an almost psychotic fear of Communist China, complicated by fallacious domino theorizing, misreadings of Asian nationalism, misplaced faith in military solutions to politico-economic problems, and an incredible series of blunders and miscalculations. All this was made even harder to bear by the facility with which the government rationalized our commitment, feeding on the nation's missionary complex to save the world from the clutches of Asian communism. Particularly distasteful was the credibility gap created by President Johnson's cabinet through the withholding and slanting of information so as to justify dispatching a spiraling number of troops and an ever higher degree of escalation.

The majority of the college-aged opposed the war on the grounds that it was unwise, unjust, and potentially dangerous for world peace. Every grandiloquent purpose for which the government claimed to be fighting was contradicted by the realities of the situation. Instead of democracy we were supporting a corrupt, dictatorial regime in South Vietnam whose claim to legitimacy, despite farcical elections, was in doubt; rather than stemming the tide of communism, we seemed to be restricting our long-range flexibility to deal with it; instead of leading to peace in Asia, the war threatened to implicate other world powers, like China, in what seemed close to turning into another world war. Even when the futility of our intervention became apparent, the government refused to begin the processes of withdrawal, arguing that the confidence of other Asian nations in the United States was at stake, an argument which ignored the fact that most of our Asian allies were already drawing up plans for their own security on the assumption that the U.S. would be in no position to become enmeshed in a second Vietnam.

Those of us who opposed the war—and the numbers were not insignificant—felt totally helpless in the face of the power of the immense government machinery to effect changes in policies. Our frustration mounted as the list of dead on both sides continued unabated, all out of proportion to our avowed purposes. Since the spontaneous and decentralized antiwar movement was unable to coalesce into one effective pressure force, there was distressingly little we could do beyond the seemingly ineffectual means available within the democratic framework: letter writing, petitioning, demonstrating, and arousing public concern and discussion.

Although I participated in all such endeavors, I was left with a terrible sense of futility and a gnawing mistrust of the high powers-that-be in government. The impact of the war, together with disturbing personal and family problems, aroused a deep sense of discontent and meaninglessness. Like my father in prewar Japan, I began having basic doubts about what I was doing, where I was headed, and why. Was there any purpose in going to graduate school, trudging along the academic treadmill, then being sent off to kill or be killed in an unjust war? Had I been born to immigrant parents who had escaped militarism in Japan, raised through bad times and good, educated in Ivy League schools, only to be placed in the jungles of Asia with rifle in hand? Was this why my parents had been disowned; why they braved the unknown to come to America—this

America now engaged in an unjustified war? For the first time in my life I thought that maybe it would have been better if they had remained in Japan.

I hit an emotional and spiritual nadir in my life. Nothing mattered anymore; nothing was important when the whole world seemed to have gone mad. I began cutting classes, skipping lectures, neglecting homework. I began pouring out pessimism and disillusionment in poems, essays, and short stories, so badly written they left me in an even deeper fit of depression. My unsettled state of mind was reflected in the inconsistent grades I received; I should have been getting all A's as a graduate student but I wasn't and furthermore did not really care. When one of my teachers at Harvard called me into his office to prod me out of my general negligence, I told him I wanted to leave graduate studies until I could straighten out my values and personal life. He agreed that it would be foolish to continue gradutae training when I was not using the opportunities of the university, and as a faculty committee also felt this way, I withdrew from graduate school, after taking my M.A., with the intention of spending two years in the Peace Corps or going abroad for study, during which time I hoped to sort out my priorities in life and gain redirection.

After dropping out of graduate school, I began to worry about being drafted for military service in Vietnam. Although at my age, twenty-six, induction seemed somewhat unlikely, I had to ask myself how I would respond to a call to duty. How would I resolve the dilemma between my strong opposition to the Vietnam war, based upon the dictates of my conscience, as against the legal responsibility of each citizen to accept the obligations of citizenship no matter how inconvenient or distasteful?

All around me were young men who actually faced this dilemma. I saw how they burned draft cards and assaulted military recruiters, and though I myself could not resort to such tactics, I understood how they felt. Many blacks summed up their own feelings about the war when they pointed out, "No Vietnamese ever called me nigger." I sympathized with their objections to risking their lives supposedly to preserve freedom and equality halfway across the globe when these same exalted ideals were often denied them at home. If I had lived my life in the ghettos, then been ordered to fight for a society that had put me there, or at least did little to help me get out, I think I too would have screamed, "Hell, no, I won't go!"

It was not a matter of being afraid to fight in a war; nor was it a pacifist's aversion for military service of any kind. While I would have preferred to remain outside military organizations, I was ready to meet my duties as an American citizen, just as I was prepared to demand all the rights granted under the Constitution. It was specifically the Vietnam War to which I objected. Hard, fundamental questions arose about the exact extent to which I was willing to carry my convictions. Would I fight? Impossible! Then what were the options? Escape across the border, renounce my U.S. citizenship and settle as an issei in Canada, just as my father had in America? Was I willing to abandon all that my parents had sacrificed to give us?

Questions arose about how loyal I felt to my country. My thoughts turned to the Daughters of the American Revolution, the John Birch Society, and all the other super-patriotic groups around the country, thoughts which forced me to face up to a painful prospect of fighting for these zealous, self-righteous jingoists. I considered the racists in society who had tried systematically to keep the Japanese oppressed. I recalled how some local chapters of the American Legion had thrown out Japanese veterans of World War I and lobbied to have all Japanese Americans herded into concentration camps. Risk my life for them? Absurd! I remembered the "red scares" of the McCarthy era, the witch-hunting, the charges of "red" and "pink," and I shuddered at the survival of primitiveness in American political thinking.

Then I also looked at the vast number of citizens who opposed the war for fundamentally the same reasons I did, and wondered why we hadn't been given some voice in the decision-making processes. Can this country be called "democratic" when vast numbers—perhaps even a majority—can be completely ignored? While we protested and demonstrated peacefully and sent letters to our elected representatives, the bombings continued, the fierce fighting did not wane, and the overall level of conflict proceded undiminished. There was even talk in military circles for a time about dropping tactical nuclear weapons on Vietnam to defoliate the jungle and end the fighting. If the U.S. government drops nuclear bombs on Vietnam, I said to myself, it will have destroyed the qualities which it claims to stand for, and I shall have no alternative but to renounce my citizenship and emigrate.

But after all the doubts and qualms were considered, when it came right down to gut questions of loyalty, I knew I felt an abiding commitment to this nation, not simply because I happened to have been born of immigrant parents but because I believe in the accumulated wisdom and historical experience that is summed up in our democratic system. Even though I disagreed with specific policies like Vietnam, the fundamental concept of democracy seemed worthy indeed of preservation and unremitting devotion.

It cannot be denied that the United States has failed to live up to all the ideals and promises of the Constitution. It has shown itself capable of great injustices and mistakes, among which the plight of racial minorities, the existence of structural imbalances, and the internment of Japanese Americans are but a few. But to impugn or reject the concept of democracy because of these shortcomings seemed basically wrongheaded. The work of redressing the ills of the society lay ahead and it did not seem right to abandon the struggle by leaving the country. The test of my own commitment to the ideals of freedom, justice, and equality would be the effort I was ready to exert to see them realized.

Moreover, for all its faults, for the immensity of the gap between myth and reality, the United States still had many redeeming virtues; it was a nation to which I felt an instinctual allegiance. It has enabled most men and women to determine their own destinies, to live without fear under the protection of individual rights, to choose the leaders they want to govern their nation. This same nation allows opponents of the war freely to air their criticisms, to attack the policies of the government, to voice protests without incurring physical sanctions. The same nation which had interned the Japanese Americans later opened up opportunities for them to rise within the system. For all their tardiness, I believe the majority of Americans do want the goals of equality and justice for all to be realized. It is an imperfect system, to be sure, but one to which I felt a deep moral commitment.

The decision to which I struggled was that in the event of induction I would carry my opposition to the war to the extent of refusing to fight though I would accept the consequences in order to maintain my citizenship. Naturally being only a cerebral decision, based on a hypothetical situation, I recognized how great the temptation for compromise would be. Even so, I felt passionate enough about the issue to carry it through.

During the process of self-examination, the striking contrast between my views and the stand taken by the thousands of nisei who had volunteered for the 442nd Infantry came to mind. How bravely they had fought, how willingly they had gone to war for a country that had put them and their families in internment camps, how much honor they had brought to the nisei name. Their loyalty and courage had paved the way for me to enjoy the full fruits of my citizenship. Yet the decision I made, though it differed greatly in content, was intended just like theirs to preserve the true ideals of democracy for which America purports to stand.

I thought too of my father and mother, of their immigration to this country and their efforts to raise us to be decent, God-fearing citizens. I wondered how they would react to the prospect of having a son imprisoned, charged with treason to their adopted nation, stripped of all voting rights, and branded an ex-criminal after release.

Shocking as it sounded, I felt confident they would understand. After all, they had raised me to decide for myself between right and wrong, and to seek the right regardless of the consequences. My father especially would have understood the dilemma I was in and would have known that I could not live without self-respect, for he too had faced such a situation and had decided against a military career. The time and countries were different but the fundamental circumstances of having to choose were not. His example gave me a sense of reassurance and strength.

In the spring of 1968, four tragic years after the decision for massive escalation, the nation prepared itself for an election. As the primaries approached, elements of the anti-Vietnam movement mobilized to make their voices heard in the critical issue before the electorate. Young students contributed positively to the movement by rallying around Eugene McCarthy, campaigning from door to door. Through their peaceful, constructive efforts McCarthy won unexpected victories in the early primary elections, bringing enormous political pressures to bear on President Johnson's Vietnam policies. Then one March evening, as I sat down to dinner before the T.V. braced to agonize through another propaganda special, I was stunned but overjoyed to hear the news: the bombing was going to be limited, Johnson was not going to run again, and steps were being speeded for peace talks.

The Johnson speech of March 31 was a victory for the millions of Americans who refused to be discouraged when their criticisms, protests, demonstrations, and other forms of opposition seemed to have no effect. The young people in particular registered a mighty impact on the nation's conscience and proved themselves to be an imposing political force with which future American presidents will have to contend.

But it was more than a triumph for young antiwar protesters. It was a victory for democracy, for the concept of government that allows popular dissent and responds to the will of the people. Finally, it was a victory for sanity and for hopes of peace. America seemed headed uncontrollably toward self-destruction, taking the rest of the world with it. Peace lovers all over the world—possessed of a desperate desire to live in spite of the world's wild careening toward doomsday—were given a faint glimmer of hope. Certainly final peace in Vietnam had not been achieved, but a critical step had been taken in that direction by stopping the dangerous escalation and assuming a willingness to curtail our military involvement.

15

Dual
Identity

AMERICA'S INTERVENTION IN VIETNAM forced me into a
painful evaluation of my political allegiances; out of the
drawn-out process of self-examination emerged a sharper
awareness of my basic commitments to, as well as responsibilities in, the realization of a truly democratic form of
government in the United States. In much the same way
my years of residence in Japan forced me into a rigorous
assessment of exactly where my personal and emotional
allegiances lay. By bringing an invaluable perspective to
my ethnic background, living in Japan helped me to
recognize, accept, and to a lesser extent resolve the
psychological neurosis with which most minority races in
America are afflicted.

Long-term residence in Japan offers certain experiences
and insights for a nisei that cannot be gained anywhere
else. The feeling of racial anonymity, for example, is something that I seldom knew in the United States. It is a joyous
sensation. How liberating to be able to amble through
crowded streets and meander down small country roads

172

with no feeling of self-consciousness about looking strange. What a relief to stride past groups of people without worrying whether one of them might suddenly point a finger at you and wisecrack, "Ah so, you are surprised I speak your language," while the rest roar with amusement. Until I lived in Japan, I never fully realized how, in the simple act of moving about in America, I was made to feel conscious of and apologetic for my race.

Becoming part of a racial mainstream in Japan was somewhat like finding the peace of mind that comes with unburdening a constant psychological cross. There were times when I was so exhilarated by the luxury of being inconspicuous that I forgot what it was like to look foreign. It was only when I saw foreign nationals subjected to rude staring that I was quickly reminded of the discomfitures of physical dissimilarity. Although my initial reactions were sympathetic toward conspicuous foreigners, I must confess that at times I derived perverse pleasure at being on the other side for a change. "Now you know what it feels like," was the thought that occasionally passed through my head.

Much as I relished my anonymity among Japanese, however, I never felt any surge of "these are my people" euphoria that some other minorities apparently experience in their motherlands. My national identity could never be Japanese, because my parents, like most other issei, had raised me to be an American—albeit one of Japanese descent. Although I may have resembled any other person in Japan, internally I was not, and probably could never be, a Japanese national. The American in me was just too strong to permit any significant degree of personal identification.

The feeling of estrangment was not, however, solely a

result of my own psychological propensities. Even if I had been more disposed to regard the Japanese as "my people," there would have been concrete obstacles interposed in any attempt to find a common identity with them —most notably the rigid insularity of this society vis-à-vis all outsiders. It is frequently and proudly said that, in contrast to the United States, no such phenomenon as racial prejudice exists in Japan; whether this is true or not —and I doubt very much that it is—I know of no country where consciousness of race is stronger than Japan. Indeed, I have never seen a people who are so prone to drawing stricter distinctions between themselves and others as the Japanese.

The term *gaijin*, a constantly heard catch-all category for all non-Japanese, is loosely translated as "foreigner." This is misleading, however, since foreigner does not begin to capture all the overt implications of gaijin. A foreigner in English is simply an alien, someone born and holding citizenship in a different country. The term does not necessarily carry racial, religious, or cultural connotations. It is a provisional category for a noncitizen, one which is no longer applicable after naturalization.

In the United States the word can designate an Asian, European, or African; a Jew, Christian, or Buddhist; a Frenchman, Nigerian, or Chinese. Since America's own heritage is a mélange of ethnic backgrounds, no one culture can be singled out as native. And because Americans are a people of immigrant stock, an aura of affection surrounds the image of the foreigner, especially since his native nation has, more probably than not, seasoned the potpourri of the nation's cultural life.

By contrast Japanese use the word gaijin to distinguish

unequivocably between "them" and "us." The accent is on the unalterable distinctiveness of those who are not Japanese. Maddening as this hard and fast emphasis may be to many nonnatives, it is perhaps understandable in the context of Japanese history and society. The flow of immigration into Japan, originating largely from the Asiatic continent, dates back to the early preagricultural era; it has been two millenniums since this large-scale influx of foreign settlers arrived. Indeed, after the start of the Edo period in 1603, the island chain was almost completely sealed off from external intercourse. For over two thousand years the country evolved into a homogeneous, insular entity, closely interwoven by a distinctive culture and social structure. Japan today is still very much an island nation. Despite its headlong plunge into international circles, it remains a closely knit, one-society, one-emperor, one-history unity which some scholars have even gone so far as to describe as one vast extended family.

Against this background the concept of gaijin takes on more pronounced nuances than just noncitizen. As suggested by the literal meaning of the characters, the word designates an "outside person," someone from outside the islands who does not fit into the social structure, a nonnative who looks quite unlike themselves, a visitor who can never, save perhaps through marriage, become a full-fledged citizen. The gaijin is, in short, virtually a different breed of man around whom the Japanese feel a definite distance and discomfort. The word encompasses the full range of racial types from hakujin and kokujin, with whom the sense of difference is keenest, to *Ajiajin* (Asians), who are physically and culturally the closest to the Japanese but with whom there is still not a sense of common identity such as exists, say, between Americans and Englishmen.

That the Japanese are keenly conscious of these distinctions is obvious in the special way they treat gaijin in Japan. Their attitudes vary from exceptional, nearly fawning kindness to irritating, at times exasperating rudeness; a natural cordiality is rather rare. Eager to project a positive image of themselves and their country, the Japanese consider it a responsibility to go out of their way to honor foreigners as *o-kyaku-san* (honored guests) of the nation. Merely being a foreigner qualifies one to be royally indulged. High-paying jobs are available, bad manners tolerated, and acquaintances easily made. Some foreigners make being a gaijin a full-time occupation, seizing all available advantages, reluctant to return to their own countries where they would lose the fringe benefits of their uniqueness. Hailing from an outside country gives many, regardless of character or ability, ready access to status, adulation, and privileges denied most Japanese themselves.

On the other hand, being a gaijin in Japan can also invite a ridicule and rudeness matched in few areas in the world. Unless they move about in protected circles, few foreign residents have escaped chafing incidents that arise with little or no provocation. Foreign males are laughed at by children, jeered at by people in passing cars, and insulted by total strangers. An annoying number of Japanese, however halting their command of conversational English, seem to possess an expressive vocabulary of profanities that are apt to fly the gaijin's way at unexpected moments. Besides being poked at and pinched, foreign females are apt to be the objects of lewd remarks, gestures, or actions. While some episodes are attributable to drunkenness, others defy rational explanation and can be accounted for only by the extraordinary consciousness of race on the part of the Japanese.

The greatest frustration of being foreign is perhaps not the sporadic outbreaks of racial antagonism so much as the distance placed between gaijin and Japanese. The gap created by the accident of birth requires concerted time and effort to close. No matter how long he may reside in Japan, how polished his command of Japanese or serviceable his knowledge of native ways, a gaijin is doomed to bear the label of outsider with all the social hindrances as well as benefits this begets. Although he may find himself surrounded by Japanese eager to make his acquaintance, he may be thwarted in seeking to press beyond the surface to form meaningful friendships. Even though he might be warmly welcomed into society, he may soon find himself at an impasse beyond which further passage is blocked, short of marriage or other inside routes. The obstructions of the Japanese social structure which confront the foreigner can make long-term residence both frustrating and lonely, turning initial infatuation into ambivalence and permanent bitterness.

Defying tidy classification, the category of nisei lies disorderly between the neat dichotomy of gaijin and *Nihonjin* (Japanese). Neither really an outsider nor fully a Japanese, the nisei is a special breed that might be dubbed semigaijin. He not was born in Japan, yet he has Japanese blood running through him. He is not a bona fide member of the social network, but he usually has relatives who are. Although he may be wholly acculturated to Western society, he is still not a total stranger to the Oriental islands of his ancestors. Japanese instinctually feel closer to a nisei than to any other category of gaijin, and it is easier for him to break into the closed society, provided of course he adapts to native ways.

There is a conscious bond that seems to put Japanese at ease in my presence. But this is apt to change abruptly if there are white or black friends around; the atmosphere, I have found, tends to become very stiff and formal. When I am shopping or dining with other foreigners, I am the one to whom store clerks and waitresses turn instinctively to talk. Even when it may be obvious that my non-Japanese companion speaks perfectly fluent Japanese, questions and answers seem inevitably to be channeled through me.

The peculiar position of the nisei is suggested by the somewhat provincial preference of the Japanese to use nisei or the term *Nikkeijin* (one of Japanese descent) over gaijin or *Amerikajin;* if the word "American" is used, it usually appears in the combined form *Nikkei-Amerikajin* (Japanese American). Even though a nisei might be as American as frozen food, from the point of view of the Japanese he is not "pure" in the same sense as a hakujin. One frequently finds, for example, advertisements in the classified section of the English-language daily *The Japan Times* such as this: "English Conversation Teachers Wanted: American, Canadian, or *nisei.*"

After meeting and talking with me, several Japanese have remarked, "What good English you speak! No trace of an accent." Although I remind them that, having been born and raised in America, this is only natural, they are still surprised. Several nisei friends in Japan have been summarily turned down for English-teaching jobs because it was feared their English was impure. One girl remarked to me, "You don't act like one, but you look just like a Japanese." "Yes, my parents are Japanese. I'm nisei," I explained. "But you look exactly like a Japanese!" she insisted. Some Japanese are conditioned to associating physical features with certain native mannerisms, and nisei, I suppose, break expected modes.

A windfall of my physical anonymity was the privacy I could enjoy. Unless I was with gaijin or drew attention to myself through other means, I could usually avoid the constant and sometimes harsh glare of public scrutiny. I was not bothered by the barrage of "May I practice my English on you?" and "How do you like Japan?" type statements to which all gaijin are subjected. My speech, one of the few clues to my nationality, unfortunately was more often than not a dead giveaway. Japanese upon hearing my accent would often gape at me as if I were illiterate. Salesgirls gawked in disbelief, then shifted into a more elementary form of Japanese, replacing stylized words like *migoto* (beautiful) with more common terms like *kirei*, and sometimes asking at the end of sentences *"Wakarimasu ka?"* (Do you understand?). One boy almost apologetically asked, "Excuse me, but what part of Japan are you from?" "I'm from America," I replied. "Ah hah." His eyes lit up. "You're nisei, aren't you? From your accent I might have guessed you to be a native of Kyushu or Shikoku." That I considered a compliment, until I heard that in some remote villages of those islands, a substantially different tongue from standard Japanese is spoken!

My anonymity worked two ways, shielding me from recognition as successfully among Japanese as among Americans. This allowed me to tune in on what Japanese said about Americans behind their backs, which could be at times hilarious, and it enabled me to witness from native eyes how some Americans in Japan behave. Unfortunately what I saw was not always cheering. Once, as I escorted two pretty Japanese girls to a park in Tokyo, a couple of boorish Americans accosted us with, *"Komban wa"* (Good evening). Smiling lecherously they asked, "You wanna have some fun tonight, girls? You wanna go to the *rowkan?"* butchering the pronunciation of *ryokan* (inn) and making me cringe with embarrassment. Although the girls kept talking, pretending not to have heard the remarks, I became irritated, particularly when the ill-bred pair refused to heed signals that their company was unwanted. No wonder Americans are so disliked abroad, I thought to myself. The two persisted: "Aw, c'mon girls, there's two of you and one of him. We'll show you a good time tonight." Having had enough, I turned around and said to one of them, "Push off, Jack. We've had all we want of your crudeness." Astonished perhaps more than intimidated, they retreated.

When Japanese discover my nationality, they are extremely curious about living conditions for Japanese abroad. The picture they have is often glossy—a life of enviable comfort and success—since the news media in Japan from time to time runs stories on the successes of the nikkeijin in North and South America. Most Japanese take vicarious pride in the achievements of the ethnic communities abroad, feeling that these accomplishments reflect on their own race and culture. They have heard about such nationally known Japanese-American politicians as Senator Daniel Inouye, Congressman Sparkie Matsunaga, and Representative Patsy Mink and are plainly pleased that persons of Japanese descent have risen so high in American politics. Numerous times Japanese have commented, "Ah, you have the same first name as Senator Inouye. What a fine name."

The Japanese often inquire about the black problem in America. They seem to have an almost morbid curiosity about the more abhorrent aspects of American life, from slaughterhouses to the drug cult, and the press carefully follows the course of race relations, often in sanctimonious tones. Although it is commendable of the Japanese that they condemn prejudice, it is easy to denounce racism when one's own society is homogeneous. One suspects a certain hypocrisy where signs of deep racial consciousness can so readily be seen. There are disquieting indications that Japan's rising nationalism might once again be expressed in terms of superiority myths.

These suspicions are bolstered when one considers how the Japanese treat other peoples. The plight of 600,000 Koreans in Japan, racially almost indistinguishable from Japanese, is disturbing evidence that a kind of discrimination as deplorable as that directed against black Americans exists. Brought over as cheap labor before and during the Second World War, the Koreans are looked down upon by many Japanese as former colonial subjects (and therefore inferior), who because they are *zurui* (wily, cunning) cannot be trusted. Faced with educational, job, and social discrimination, barred from citizenship despite birth in Japan, the Koreans have been forced to eke out livelihoods on standards well below those of Japanese, accepting low-paying jobs and often living in wretched urban ghettos.

Nor, despite disclaimers, are the Japanese guiltless of color prejudice. Eurasian children are not always accepted in Japanese circles and the treatment accorded Negro-Japanese can be cruel. Ostracized from society and discriminated against because of the dark color of their skin, many find themselves in a position similar to that of black

Americans not long ago: shut off from desirable jobs, only a few being able to break into lucrative occupations such as the entertainment field. Because of intolerant attitudes toward "impure" children, these unfortunate young people face a serious identity problem. Japanese may wax indignant over the black crisis, but they have yet to face up to their own version of color discrimination, which is in many ways as ruthless as that directed against black people in America. Doubters need only ask Negro-Japanese children or Korean residents whether racial prejudice exists or not in Japan.

Of all categories of outsiders, nisei are probably the only group to escape both the extreme type of overt discrimination that is reserved for Negro-Japanese and Koreans and the more covert racial distinctions that are drawn in the case of other foreigners. Yet perhaps due to this sense of closeness, the Japanese can be more acid in their criticisms of nikkeijin when there is a failure to conform to native standards of propriety. Nisei are expected to be familiar with Japanese ways. "He should know better; after all his parents are Japanese," is a comment I have frequently heard. For this reason alone it rarely happens that, despite the lack of racial rancor, Japanese Americans are able easily to make the transition into Japanese society. Successful adjustment often means suppressing the American element in the nisei's personality; since most of those born in the States are dominantly American in personality, they often find long-term residence in Japan uncomfortable. Neither able nor willing to become fully Japanese, they sometimes incur harsh indictment for having lost their Asian heritage.

Moreover, the Japanese are sometimes capable of

becoming rather arrogant toward nisei, particularly over the question of immigration. Issei hailed largely from poor farming families along the Inland Sea area—Shikoku, Hiroshima, Kyushu, and even as far as Okinawa. Most were second and third sons who, by rigid rules of primogeniture, were barred from inheriting family land; finding their lot hard and opportunities scanty, many were forced to emigrate as a desperate resort, with the intention of returning to Japan after making their fortunes. Their adjustment to America under such duress was truly remarkable, a proud testimony to the strengths of the agricultural areas of Japan. Their industry and ingenuity were reflections of the traditional vitality of the agrarian sector—the base upon which Japan's swift takeoff into modern industrial growth was launched.

But some Japanese belittle the nisei offspring of these immigrants because of their humble origins. They obviously consider issei a group that just could not make it in Japan. If issei had remained, some think, they would have stayed at the bottom of society; abroad they had good fortune and greater opportunities to rise. Questions are occasionally put to me in tones of dizzying condescension—"What do your parents do?" "Where do they come from in Japan?" "Did they attend college?"—by Japanese anxious to pin class labels on me. It is put even more pointedly by some: "Are your parents farmers?" Curiously, Japanese who phrase questions with such uncharacteristic indelicacy are usually the same ones who look upon life abroad with the greatest envy.

Slights are rare and inconsequential, however, when weighed against the advantages of having relatives living in Japan. In contrast to Caucasian visitors who often complain about never being invited into native homes, most nisei find doors to Japanese familes wide open. If anything, the complaint heard most often is that they are asked into Japanese homes too much, especially by relatives. The obligation of making the rounds to pay respects to relatives can be time consuming, yet relatives represent the most rewarding aspect of being a nisei in Japan. They provide an avenue into the extended family social structure where the real Japan can be experienced, in addition to offering the kind of warm fellowship that flows from the gathering of kin.

Because my parents departed for the United States after severing their network of family ties, I grew up feeling deprived of the childhood delights customarily associated with large numbers of in-laws. There were no kindly uncles or aunts to take me to football games, no rambunctious cousins to play with, and no family reunions to anticipate. All I knew was my immediate family. Whenever I asked about relatives, my parents, who had lost touch during the war, had very little to relate. Correspondence was sporadic at best and many of our closest kin, particularly on my father's side, had been killed in combat. I arrived in Japan therefore with only a few names and addresses of relatives, having the barest sketch of family genealogy.

Although my maternal in-laws were at Haneda airport to welcome me, my initial contact with my paternal relatives came when I visited a cousin in Iwakuni. This, the first of a series of trips all over Japan, brought into clear focus certain blurred images that had been formed on the basis of imagination and irregular correspondence. This cousin, who had always seemed little more than an abstraction, suddenly became animated—a real person—when a voice inquired behind me at Iwakuni station, *"Iwao-san desu ka?"* It was the first time anyone had called me by my Japanese name and for an interval it did not register. Then, realizing the unfamiliar words were intended for me, I turned around to see the tall, gaunt figure of my cousin standing before me. He was not at all as I had pictured him. He was a former Army colonel who had seen extensive service in the Pacific, and I had quite a different idea, taken from war movies, of what he might look like. But he was slender, almost bony, kindly, and of gentle disposition. His facial features, though longer, resembled my father's and it was thrilling to be reminded of my father in the land he knew as a child.

The family lavished hospitality upon me that exceeded the wildest dictates of family duty. Taking time off from work, they guided me around the area, introduced me to old friends of my father, dressed me in Japanese clothes for the local O-bon Festival, and initiated me into traditional rural life. Instead of more sight-seeing I insisted upon following what for them was a normal day's routine, including back-breaking hours out in the fields, followed by baths in their huge, old, round, stone tub filled with water so scalding that I could hardly poke my toe in, still less immerse myself. The days ended with leisurely dinners for which, much against my protests, the family went far beyond their means to feast me with gargantuan servings of fish, vegetables, and rice. In the remaining hours after dinner we all sat around absorbed in conversation about the Okimoto family tree and the American members' lives.

From these relatives I received a comprehensive history of my ancestry, learning for the first time just how unusual my parents' backgrounds were. Since neither my father nor mother had alluded much to their lives in Japan, I was greatly surprised to learn of the details of their early years, expulsion from home, and immigration abroad. Pictures looking as if they had been taken in another century were pulled out of dusty albums, including one of my parents' wedding; my young, dark, intense father stood above my mother who, richly clad in a kimono, sat with her hands resting demurely in her lap, looking of all things like a geisha with her enormous black wig, white powdered skin, and tiny cherry plum of a mouth. Never had I seen my God-fearing mother in kimono, let alone thickly powdered or with lipstick! One eighty-eight-year-old haiku-writing relative, who was quite the raconteur as he sat on the tatami floor, legs crossed, smoking hand-rolled cigarettes, laughing merrily like some figure out of a Hiroshige woodblock print, wove fascinating tales about Tameichi-kun (my father), adding emphasis here and there by the animated movements of bushy white eyebrows that resembled the downward flap of wings.

The week in Iwakuni also revealed a Japan very unlike the one I had known in Tokyo. It brought me into agrarian areas, the last repositories of the old Japan, introducing aspects of a great tradition that is rapidly undergoing change in the hectic flurry of industrialization and urbanization. Vestiges of old customs, glimpses of traditional social patterns, profiles of the lovely natural landscape that has inspired some of the world's most elegant poetry, the simple unaffected kindness of the rural people are memories of the countryside I shall always cherish. What I saw of this Japan made me proud that generations of habitation on these islands were somehow part of my own past.

Perhaps the most moving incident of this memorable

week came as I stood on the tiny plot of land which, were it not for one decision, might have been the source of my family's livelihood. The magnitude of my father's choice to emigrate dawned on me with full force. How inconceivable would have been the differences, I mused, had my father not possessed the restlessness and courage to break with land and nation. The temptation to choose the easy road of security and certainty must have been great, but thanks to his determination to find a more meaningful life, we were all raised on another continent, the unknowing and all too often ungrateful heirs of his spirit of adventure. Suddenly I was sharply conscious of what I had always taken for granted: birth and life in America.

The small plot—the same my father had rejected—was like an old but undiscovered promontory from which I could gaze clearly into an uncharted area of my life that had been previously hidden in a thick mist of ignorance. Like most nisei I had lived exclusively, until that moment, in a linear world of the present and future. By returning to the cradle of my Asian ancestry whole new horizons were revealed, opening up a world of an eastern past that gave my perspective on life three-dimensional fullness.

This sudden awareness of my family's past proved therapeutic for the chronic problem of schizophrenic identity with which I have been struggling. Living in Japan made me conscious, as nothing else could have, of being very much an American in my personal attitudes and tastes. Yet, at the same time, it liberated me from distasteful notions, compounded by ignorance, that had been associated with Japan and my ethnic past. In America I could define to my satisfaction just how willing I was to acknowledge the Asian background in me. By turning racial ethnicity into a poisonous source of self-contempt, society had instilled in me a sense of shame, at times flaring into self-pity and self-hatred, for being a hyphenated American. Although feelings of profound ambivalence will probably never be permanently settled, at least most of the fundamental uncertainties about my ethnic heritage have been resolved. Indeed, it was only after spending several years in my ancestral homeland that I could acknowledge the Japaneseness in me without embarrassment or apology. And it was not until I accepted my ethnic heritage that I could reply without hesitation or uneasiness to the question "What are you?"—I am Japanese American, not someone in disguise.

16

Women, Race, and Marriage

IN CONTRAST TO MOST ISSEI parents, who actively encourage their children to find brides within the Japanese-American community or from Japan, my parents almost never expressed any preferences, because it was their feeling that marriage is a very personal matter, transcending neat racial or social categories, in which the two parties involved are best fit to make the final decision free from parental interference. Though I always suspected they secretly wanted me to marry a Japanese, I was never given any heart-to-heart talks about the desirability of maintaining the "purity" of our race. What reservations I had about interracial matches were due primarily to disagreeable episodes arising out of interracial dating.

Perhaps the only time my parents ever sat me down for a parent-to-child session was on the eve of my departure for Tokyo, and it was less a lecture on marriage than a precautionary briefing on how not to behave in Japan. Fundamentalist Christian ministers that they were, my parents were really quite concerned about the carnal temptations of living in Tokyo. My mother, trying hard to be low-keyed, but visibly nervous at the thought of her last son walking into the world's largest capital—a city notorious for its sensual enticements—sought to exact pledges that I would not wander into the vast terrain of the *mizu shobai* (entertainment world). Yes, yes, I assured her, my time was much too valuable to waste on any but girls from "good families." My father was also concerned. "I hear modern Japanese girls, even some *ojosan* (well-bred ladies from good families) act immodestly these days, using heavy make-up, wearing unchaste clothes, and running shamelessly after boys. As a nisei you must be especially careful, for many girls think all Americans are rich and may chase after you."

I took my parents' solemn words of warning rather lightheartedly, not letting them dampen my enthusiasm over the prospect of meeting a great variety of Japanese women. After several years in the cloistered confines of an all-male college I was not adverse to some adventure, a few existential experiences, and if it happened to work out, perhaps the growth of a romance. Little did I anticipate what cultural shocks lay in store.

My first date with a Japanese girl—for all parental fears and personal expectations—turned out intolerably dull. Having asked out an ojosan whose background my parents would have found impeccable, I met her in one of the many coffee houses in Shibuya. Unwittingly, I thought that a quiet evening of conversation would be the quickest way to get to know her. But try as I might I could not get the conversation off the ground. Clumsiness in Japanese may have been a factor but I think it was due more to the disinclination of the girl to carry her portion of the conversation. Every time I introduced a new topic the girl would answer in monosyllables. Sitting shyly across from me, eyes modestly lowered, she responded to questions by raising her eyes, forcing out a soft *hai* (yes), an *iie* (no), or a profound *so desu ne* . . . (well . . .), then lowering her gaze again. Or she would just sit there and giggle.

It is the general practice of Japanese girls not to press their opinions forward in the presence of boys. Although stimulating thoughts may be passing through their heads, most girls are reluctant to verbalize them for fear of sounding too aggressive. Needless to say this is a sharp contrast to American girls, who will express their views freely, even challengingly, before boys. Japanese men seem to prefer their women to mute their ideas; overly talkative or intelligent types are considered *ammari onnarashiku nai* (not very feminine). Since someone who is ready to interject opinions may represent a threat to masculine pride, a woman is feminine only when she stays within the accepted role assigned her—namely intellectual humility. As a result some of the most interesting women I have met in Japan have had to forgo the usual aspirations of marriage and children; not many men are willing to wed those who shatter established roles in order to develop their minds or pursue professional careers.

Although the Japanese woman is gaining greater latitude of movement, old images of feminine domesticity are slow in dying. Japanese men, even the modern young, still seek wives who can find fulfillment in the home. The ideal girl is one who is faithful and efficient, a good housekeeper and mother, a pillar of support for her mate. Independent women, no matter how beautiful or talented, who do not want to spend their lives in a kitchen are not considered suitable wife material. Hence the qualities that are most often sought include good health, gentleness, obedience, faithfulness, domestic efficiency—in short, someone *Nihonteki* (typically Japanese) who will look after her husband for the whole of her life.

Dating is a postwar phenomenon, imported from the West but looked upon somewhat differently by the Japanese. Sometimes it is a chance for boys and girls to get together in groups for casual companionship. More often it is an opportunity, as in America, for starry-eyed couples to spend time getting to know each other. Dating in the latter sense is taken far more seriously by Japanese than American girls, especially if more than one date is involved. I once committed the blunder of asking out a pretty coed three times in the space of two months without realizing what significance she attached to such "regular" dating. For the fourth date she invited me to her home for dinner— an invitation which, not commonly extended, I was delighted to accept.

Until I reached her home I was quite eager to meet her family. But I sensed trouble the minute they sat me in the center of their living room and from an enclosed circle fired a volley of questions about my background and future ambitions. Asked what I wanted to do, I replied that I was considering a teaching career. "Oh wonderful," exclaimed the father, "I've always wanted my sons to go into something academic." This prompted me to add hastily that the foreign service was another possibility—to which the mother replied, "Wouldn't it be nice to have a diplomat in the family?" When the grilling session ended the parents pulled out pictures of their daughter to show what a "healthy" girl she was and how many fine, strong children she could bear. It was all I could do to suppress a sickly claustrophobic desire to leap up and run. When hints were dropped about writing my parents to discuss a "suitable arrangement," disconcerting visions of my father and mother dropping from heart attacks upon reading the letter of proposal leapt to mind and I somehow managed to muster enough wit to fabricate an excuse to leave immediately. As innocent as our three dates had been, the frequency had apparently convinced the family that I harbored long-range designs on their daughter. Had I been an ordinary foreigner, perhaps the occasion might not have arisen; in fact the parents might have tried to discourage the girl from seeing any more of me. But because I was of Japanese descent, the parents had confided, they could feel assured their daughter would be properly looked after.

It is curious that in spite of the petrified and sometimes unkind racial distinctions that are drawn, many foreign nationals of hedonistic bent find Japan an Oriental Babylon of pleasure. Japanese are said to be *yowai* (weak, vulnerable) toward gaijin, who seem to exude charm by virtue of a romanticized image. In contrast to some nisei girls who prefer to choose their men from the Japanese-American community, not a few Japanese women are attracted by the mystique surrounding foreigners. Gaijin men for the most part are not apt to let such opportunities pass. "I've never been in a country where the girls are easier to make," commented one foreign "scholar" who spent four years ostensibly studying in Tokyo and boasts of having slept with several hundred girls.

Being nisei, I do not attract the hordes of good-time

girls that flock after conspicuous gaijin. When I walk into coffee shops or go-gos few girls pay me more than passing heed. But because I am Western by nationality and up-bringing, I am sometimes stuck with the whole romantic syndrome connected with being foreign. Once my true identity is found out, I become the object of rather explicit interest. Some girls get that faraway look in their eyes; others stare at me as if I represented a free air ticket to America. One girl in a crowded smoke-filled coffee house, upon discovering my nationality, bowled me over with a blunt question that perked up ears for tables around: "Have you slept with a Japanese girl yet?" Another ultra-mod type, turning on a Marlene Dietrich look, asked point blank, "I hear nisei are terribly passionate. Is it true? Are you one of the wildly passionate kind?"

For a boy who grew up protected from the allurements of the world and was steeped in the puritanical tradition, such Dionysian jolts to my morality necessitated radical adjustments in my mental attitudes. From childhood into late adolescence, my basic notions of morality were molded primarily by a conservative brand of Christianity. Every day I memorized and attempted to embody moral precepts from the New Testament. No matter what the situation, I could quote appropriate verses to serve as guidelines for behavior.

Thanks to this thorough inculcation of Christian ethics, strict distinctions between the flesh and the spirit were ingrained in my thinking, always in the dualistic form of the corporeal being evil and the spiritual good. Human life consisted of a titanic struggle between forces of the spirit against the temptations of the flesh. Morality was the triumph of mind over body, the conquest of asceticism over gratification. Maintaining purity was a full-time occupation that called for the continual suppression of sinful, animalistic cravings for sex.

The Bible is replete with tales about the terrible sin of sexual license, beginning with Genesis and the Original Sin of Adam and Eve. The letters of the apostle Paul, which I was fond of reading, unequivocally state that it is best to remain a pure ascetic, but if one simply cannot live without sex it is better to marry than burn in hell. The message is clear: sex is an intrinsically degrading act, legitimate only in marriage, outside of which it is cause for eternal damnation in the fiery furnace of hell.

In Japan I was mystified by attitudes toward sex and love that are so alien to the precepts on which I was raised. Of course morality in Japan, as in America, is in a state of revolutionary transition with generational gaps growing seemingly wider each year. But to understand how the Japanese have traditionally viewed ethics I had to divest my mind of all ingrained concepts of Christian thought. Even though my attitudes represented an extreme, I found that social values and traditions in Japan are not generally amenable to Western categories of analysis and must be accepted on their own terms.

Sex in old Japan was regarded primarily as a physical phenomenon. With a double standard long in operation, sex for women was a marital means of procreation; for men it was a physical pleasure to be liberally enjoyed either inside or outside marriage with no intrinsic opprobrium. In the traditional code of ethics, sex constituted a distinct province in life, bearing no necessary relationship to love or emotional involvement. It was like eating or sleeping: a function of the human body. As Ruth Benedict has pointed out in *The Chrysanthemum and the Sword,* the Japanese "consider physical pleasures good and worthy of cultivation. They are sought and valued."

Japanese morality was hence unfettered by Christian concepts of sin and guilt; no Augustinian dualism of sex/evil, spirit/good dominated ethical thought. Yet the absence of sin did not mean the Japanese were wholly given over to sexual debauchery; some social mechanisms of control existed. What restrained desire from turning into license were social obligations and certain standards of propriety. The restrictions were particularly inhibiting for women, who had to maintain chaste decorum, but some strict regulations were imposed on male behavior as well. Sex was fine, a pleasure to be cultivated almost as an art, but it was to be kept in perspective at all times. Never was it to become a consuming obsession that might cause the neglect of social commitments. Whenever sex threatened to interfere with the fulfillment of higher obligations—to family, friends, superiors, job—it was to be stringently controlled. Failure to meet obligations on account of sexual excesses brought shame on oneself. Since shame was as dreaded by Japanese as guilt was by Westerners, sensual indulgence was kept under control.

Because of its relative standards of moral judgment, Japanese society has been, and still is, considerably more tolerant of a variety of bodily drives than Judeo-Christian culture. Since it was assumed that men had natural needs that had to be met, procuring the services of professionals in flourishing amusement quarters was permissible, if not expected, so long as patronage did not drain family finances or endanger social commitments. Men did not have to sneak around furtively to satisfy their desires. Nor was homosexuality regarded, as in the West, as an abnormality or sickness. Male homosexual relationships were accepted without recrimination and even today liberal attitudes are suggested by the popularity of self-confessed homosexuals and male transvestites in the entertainment field. Their public ratings are not harmed in the least by their offbeat views on sex.

Like so many other facets of postwar Japan traditional moral codes seem to be in the process of change. The young today no longer adhere to values and practices that characterized male-female relations before the war. For a growing number of Japanese women the notion of a double standard of morality—a liberal one for males and a severely restricted one for females—is losing popularity as the social disparity between sexes is gradually narrowed. In keeping with the redefinition of traditional roles, young Japanese housewives are demanding, and perhaps getting, more fidelity from their spouses. If their husbands neglect them or play with other women, some wives may seek divorce or perhaps retaliate with what had previously been taboo: extra-marital sex. The number of *yoromeki dorama* (TV soap operas dealing with adulterous affairs), articles in weekly magazines dealing with unfaithfulness, and scores of cartoons depicting illicit relations are chronicles of the shifting standards of behavior. Divorces are on the rise, as are expectations of fulfillment through marriage, and although it would be hasty to predict a thoroughgoing Westernization of sex, love, and marriage on the basis of recent short-term trends, it does seem likely that with climbing prosperity, increasing leisure, and the evolving social structure, traditional values will be permanently changed.

Already there are signs of basic changes in such institutions as marriage. Before the war, marriages were arrangements worked out by parents on the basis of such family considerations as lineage, status, occupation, and advantageous connections; the children were hardly consulted at all. Since the war, however, couples now have at least as important a say in the matter as their parents and increasingly they are basing their choice on emotional rather than familial factors. Whether it be traditional *o-miai* (arranged) or modern *renai* (love) matches, love is assuming increasing importance both before and after the ceremony. A unique combination of o-miai and renai systems presently exists in which couples will consent to arranged meetings to get things started, but will maintain the final right to refuse a marriage if either party feels the prospect of love is remote.

Several times during my stay in Tokyo, friends and relatives sent me feelers about going through several informal o-miai meetings. It was inevitable that the prospective female was given a superlative buildup by acquaintances offering to act as *nakodo* (matchmakers) in making the necessary arrangements. Impressive as the data on the eligible young lady sounded, I always rejected the well-intended offers, not just to avoid the web of human relations that threatened to entangle me if I consented to a meeting, but more centrally, because the very idea of having a marriage "arranged" for me struck my sensibilities as offensive. Once it was understood that the very notion of an o-miai went against certain ingrained American preferences, all the probings ceased.

Rejection of the Japanese system of finding a spouse, however, in practice imposed rather strict limitations on the field of marital candidates among Japanese women. Of course the American style of dating and deciding was by no means a blind alley; any number of nisei and gaijin, not to mention Japanese, follow the American route to marriage. However, it was my experience that real obstacles stood in the way of getting to know Japanese women well enough to make a firm decision, because whenever I began to get acquainted with certain prospects, our relationships were always complicated by the intrusion of premature pressures to marry. It was almost as if marriage were the precondition of becoming close, not the reverse as in the West. Courting meant getting ensnarled in a tangle of family ties and obligations that were definitely not worth the rewards of the pursuit. As attractive as I found Japanese girls, therefore, I was never willing to put up with either the practices or pressures of the society in seeking one out for a bride.

Among American girls my dating habits were quite diversified. Choices for social companions ran the racial gamut from white to black and spanned the ethnic range from Chinese to Jewish. In dating I tried consciously not to let racial factors enter into consideration, but if I am honest, I must confess that it was much easier to socialize with nisei than nonnisei because I didn't have to assume the social and psychological risks of trespassing on someone else's racial territory. With Japanese-American females there was a shared background of experiences and origins that took much of the strain out of dating. It was a relief, among other things, not to have to worry whether my date's parents would disapprove of her stepping out with a nisei. I tried to mingle widely with nisei girls on the West Coast, becoming serious enough about two to consider marriage, but the disadvantage of circulating only within the subculture was that there were so few of them. By restricting myself solely to the nisei community, I was severely limiting my range of choices and in view of this it is perhaps not surprising that I was frustrated in my hopes to find just the right wife among Japanese Americans.

This led me to date with other races at least as extensively as with Japanese. But socializing outside my race was not always easy. I felt viscerally knotted up at times in the company of non-Japanese, upset as much by my own ambivalences as by the existence of concrete social barriers. Although liberalizing slowly, the social atmosphere in America is still strongly hostile to interracial matches. The stares, the jeers, the cold shoulders, the feigned approval are but a small part of the underlying social opprobrium connected with racial intermixing, or "mongrelization," as some detractors are fond of calling it.

Interracial socializing was complicated in my own mind by the fact that I had grown up in a society in which white standards represented the highest criterion of judgment. In this white-dominated society, it was perhaps natural that white girls seemed attractive personally as well as physically. They were in a sense symbols of the social success I was conditioned to seek, all the more appealing, perhaps, because of the subtly imposed feelings of self-derogation associated with being a member of a racial minority. In the inner recesses of my heart I resisted the seductive attraction of white girls because I feared I was being drawn to them for the wrong reasons. I was afraid that my tastes had been conditioned too centrally by white standards. Behind the magnetism there may have been an unhealthy ambition to prove my self-worth by competing with the best of the white bucks and winning the fair hand of some beautiful, blue-eyed blonde—crowning evidence of having made it.

Such suspicions were aggravated by deep-seated resentment and fear: resentment against feeling compelled to prove myself in the white world to begin with, and fear of failing or being hurt by prejudice in the process. All of this rendered me unable to look upon my relationships with white women with the same degree of objective equanimity that I could with others. At times I felt helplessly caught in the turmoil of conflicting feelings of attraction and repulsion, love and hate. The closer I drew to white girls, it seemed, the tighter I tended to close up and the more turbulent became my feelings.

The repetition of some unpleasant encounters accounted largely for the internal tensions and the depth of defensiveness with which I looked upon white womanhood. One of my closest high school friends, for example, to whom I confided an interest in a particular girl, commented, "But she's an American," implying that I had no business or right trying to see her. College classmates were generally tolerant, but even some of them frowned when I was with white dates; many, trying to be helpful, annoyed me by such statements as "Hey, there's a cute Chinese chick at Vassar," or "Let me set you up with this Japanese babe at Wellesley" in tones that suggested whites were the sole preserve of other whites. Perhaps if I had been surer of my own dual identity I would have been less sensitive about such comments.

What I dreaded most of all was meeting the white families of my dates. The redundance of humiliating experiences made me incapable of approaching the front door of a home without some degree of trepidation. Younger brothers have come to the door and yelled, "Hey, Sis, Mr. Moto is here." Although, fortunately, I never faced parents on rocking chairs with shotguns in hand, I was greeted by one mother who rushed out cursing and screaming at me to stay away from her daughter or she would call the police. While more restrained, some fathers have resorted to more subtle but equally cutting ways to make it perfectly clear that my interest in their fair-haired daughters would not be encouraged. Even when, as was usually the case, parents tried very hard to welcome me as they would any other escort, the kind of questions they asked and the efforts to appear broadminded were no more than thin veneers of politeness. It is nearly impossible to count the number of times I've been told, "Oh, we visited Japan and just loved it. The people there are so nice. The countryside is so neat and the gardens, oh the gardens, are superbly beautiful." While kindly intended, the facile implication of such statements was of course that a nisei is not American, but a Japanese. When the condescension became too much, I was not above answering in kind, "Yes, there isn't anyone that can take care of gardens like us Japanese. We may not be as good as you whites, but we sure know how to tend our gardens."

Most of the inhospitable treatment, however, was really unnecessary because I seldom allowed myself to get involved romantically with white girls. Whether deliberately or subconsciously, I seemed to cut off ties before the question of marriage came up. Or I sometimes undermined relations by taking an antagonistic attitude. Racial questions were raised eventually and even though the willingness of girls to go out with me should have been ample evidence of freedom from bias, I was driven at times to test the authenticity of their liberalism through pointed interrogation.

It was only through the refusal of one white girl to be deterred by all my defense mechanisms that I finally overcame the deep-seated suspicions that years of racial antagonisms had implanted. Her name, Nancy Miller, sounded about as ill-matched for mine as her whole background and personality seemed utterly unsuited for a complicated, sometimes angry Japanese American. She was from a middle-class, Anglo-Saxon family in Idaho, one far removed from consciousness of racial tensions.

When we began dating, all my latent suspicions toward white women came rushing out. I questioned her motives in going out with a Japanese American, because I was wary of those who thought socializing in minority circles was "in." I turned down invitations to visit her family in Idaho because I was wrongly afraid of receiving cold treatment. I provoked her into arguments over the black-power movement, interpreting anything below my level of emotional militancy as signs of an inability to understand the wounded self-respect and fury of the black people. The more serious we became, it seemed, the more frantically I searched for ways to ward off the impending, inescapable question of marriage.

As the prospect of an interracial marriage loomed larger, my own feelings became hopelessly confused and vacillating. On the one hand my love for her was deep, yet I could not decide whether it would withstand the assault of racial and cultural problems that would certainly arise. Nor, deep down, could I rid myself of the suspicion that my parents preferred to have a Japanese daughter-in-law.

Not long after I left for Japan, Nancy, at my request, flew to Tokyo not only to be near me but to become familiar with the culture that was an integral part of my identity. She embarked upon an intense study of the language, history, arts, and cuisine and, according to Japanese friends, was Japanized in many of her habits and mannerisms. In time she became as conversant in the culture as anyone in my family, thus eliminating whatever cultural obstacles stood in the way of the fulfillment of our relationship.

But, even with one problem settled, the major problem, that of race, still lingered. Though I wanted very much to forget the racial issue, old doubts haunted me in both conscious and subconscious ways. I had a series of disturbing dreams that were variations on a central theme: white cruelty toward Japanese. Although I dismissed the first few sequences as remnants of unwarranted fears of being hurt by prejudice, when they persisted I began to worry that racial apprehensions had been so permanently drummed into my thought processes that there was no way I could enter into an untroubled marriage outside my race. I was furious at the racism that had contaminated our relationship and I hated myself for not possessing the largeness of spirit to rise above it all.

At the height of my uncertainty, my father happened to send me a letter which provided the wisdom and perspective I so desperately needed. It was a letter, written in Japanese, which coincided perfectly not only with my own marital indecision but, significantly, with the celebration of the one-hundredth year of Japanese immigration to America. In it my father expressed thoughts I already believed intellectually but whose truths I had to hear directly from him to accept emotionally. He said that no decision of importance—certainly not one which would affect my life as much as marriage—was ever easy; there would always be an element of uncertainty. But I should not be paralyzed by doubts about minor turns and curves if I was certain about the basic direction in which I wanted to head. Because he had experienced serious misgivings about leaving for America, he sympathized with some of the fears I was struggling to cope with. But just as any adventure required the acceptance of certain risks, the search for fulfillment in love called for trust and courage and effort, three qualities without which life would be singularly unrewarding. With candidness and paternal affection, he revealed that although he might at one time have preferred a Japanese daughter-in-law for the sheer ease of communication, as far as he and my mother were concerned they could not ask for a finer person for their last son than Nancy. In fact, he went on, when he crossed the Pacific to settle in America, he intended his children to grow up as Americans, not Japanese, and because of my own acculturation to American society I would probably be happier and better suited to marry a Caucasian than a Japanese. In any case, love was a matter of the heart and soul, not of culture and race, and as long as we had that and were willing to work to keep it, there was no reason our marriage could not overcome whatever social obstacles might arise and be every bit as fulfilling as he wished for us. In a final sentence that typified his unwavering devotion as a father, he assured me that whatever my decision I would have his blessing.

My father died a few weeks after sending this letter. He never lived to know what impact his letter—indeed his whole life—had on me. It was just the fatherly assurance I needed to take Nancy unreservedly as my wife. My only regret was that he could not have attended the wedding he himself had encouraged and blessed. The wedding ceremony, like those of my two brothers, took place where the story of my parents' immigration started: in Japan. Nancy and I were both exceedingly happy to be joined together in the land where my parents, just three short decades before had taken their vows before embarking upon the journey to America.

It was probably no accident that the decision to marry, as well as the ceremony itself, took place in Japan, because it was only after I had spent several years in my ancestral homeland that I could accept myself with a dual identity. The struggle to be recognized as a "normal" American at the expense of suppressing the Japanese in me, as well as the periodic swings into rage against white Americans, ceased troubling me so much after I had accepted the fact that I am Japanese American. In looking ahead there could very well be similar problems of identity for my children, perhaps compounded by the actual mixing of races. Although my wife and I can do little to influence the basic treatment that awaits our children in American society, we can try to provide them with the option of learning about, and perhaps accepting, the rich Asian legacy that is theirs to inherit so that they need not feel apologetic, as I have for most of my life, for their dual identity. It will be somewhat different for them than it was for me. Physically, at least, half the disguise I have worn will be lost; emotionally, I hope the day will come when they and all my country's racial minorities are no longer made to feel any less American because of their ethnic heritage.

The "weathermark"
identifies this book as having been
planned, designed, and produced at
John Weatherhill, Inc.
7-6-13 Roppongi, Minato-ku, Tokyo 106
Book design and typography by Ronald V. Bell
Composition by Samwha Printing Co., Seoul
Printing by Kenkyusha Printing Co., Tokyo
Bound at the Makoto Binderies, Tokyo
Type used is 12-point Monotype Baskerville
with hand-set Optima Bold for display